#THREADING STARS

ANTI-CRISIS LETTERS

BY

VAN RAY PARKER

EXPANDSION OF THE STARS OF FATE STARFLAKES

SERIES OF PROSE, ART, AND CRAFTS

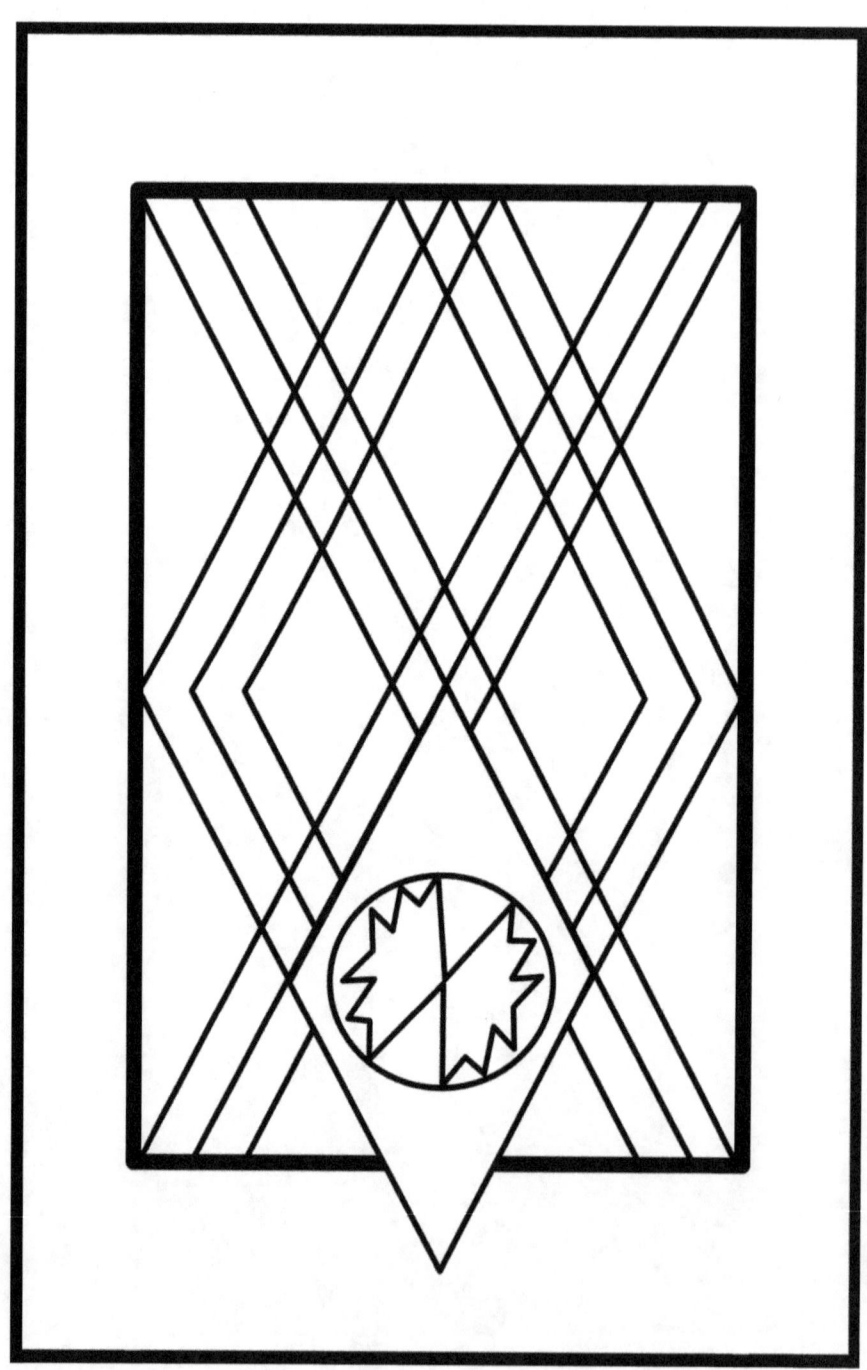

Chapter and Titles
#Threading Stars

Contents

EXPANDSION OF THE STARS OF FATE STARFLAKES SERIES OF PROSE, ART, AND CRAFTS
Books and Other Projects

Rainbow Starflake

The Prose Poems in narrative imagery

Art Plaques- bringing together the prose poems and the Stars of Fate Starflakes together

Kirigami Starflakes

Anti- Crisis Coloring Journals

Art Themes- Social Exhibition Themes

Anti-Crisis Letters / Letters of Hope and Light-

Anti-Racism Crisis Letters- short stories and prose poems

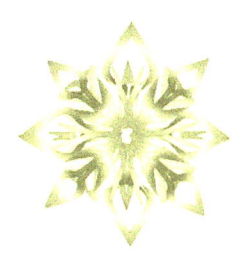

Artistic Statement-Van Ray Parker

# #

The Stars of Fate, Starflakes are different parts of feelings that are expressed with two interwoven shapes representing the strength of character and expression of emotion, to most they look like snowflakes or do not look anything like snowflakes. The Letters of Hope and Light the *Anti-Crisis Letters* are sent with the *Stars of Fate Starflakes* wrapped around words to help inspire or help repair, or in times an answer to a suicide letter that could not be given in return and can be sympathetic greeting cards with a Kirigami crafted Starflakes.

The *Anti-Crisis Letters* are a symbol for individuals to seek help or to write a letter for help and expression, not a suicide letter, a way of thought to offer more than the suicide letter and change the dynamic of writing a suicide letter to turn it to a Letter of Hope and Light the *Anti-Crisis letter*. The individuals that want to write a suicide letter to write for hope to move forward to get past what is making their life feeling unbearable to keep living or writing a letter to someone that was lost and cannot be given a letter from loved ones. In different themes mediums are used in various ways to bring together each of the Starflakes with narrative prose, letters, or statements written as Anti-Crisis Letters. The different ways of cutting the Stars of Fate Starflakes and the *Anti-Crisis Letters* that reflect what the Starflakes were to convey with different visual themes or grouping of Starflakes, all to have an underlying theme of prevention of suicide.

#ThreadingStars is a hashtag used across social media to categorize the Starflakes and the Prose I write.

;

The form of the Anti-Crisis letter Prose is in two parts a statement and then a clarifying statement, in most cases separated by a semicolon.

Mission Statement

Turning an act of lethal intent to asking for help or giving comfort with words to heal and turning symbols of Starflakes into hopeful points of contact.

Social Exhibition Themes

Theme- SHADOW STARFLAKES

The theme of Shadow Starflakes is a specific way of cutting the Stars of Fate Starflakes (Fated Starflakes) that when cut and two shapes interwoven then held up to light the Starflakes is the shadow in the center, representing hidden issues like mental health and mood disorder issues.

Theme- KINDHEARTED PASTEL

Bringing awareness to social issues, and cultural awareness with the Ant-Racism Crisis Letters

Theme- PARADISE STARFLAKES

problem-solving statement restatement techniques. Paradise Starflakes are translucent colored Starflakes, the two interwoven Kirigami colored shapes filter to make a different color

Theme- STARFLAKES PRIDE

Mixed Colorful Stars of Fate Starflakes with parallel landscape Anti-Crisis Plaques with prose written from journal entries to make Letters of Hope and Light for inspiration and encouragement finding independent narratives, and pride in life to form bonds or opening a dialog.

Theme- STARFLAKES JOURNEY

A constellation of the Stars of Fate Starflakes with Geo- Animal Starflakes and flora and fauna Starflakes on black canvas or black background

with a connection to the other exhibit themes

Bringing together *Starflakes and Anti-Crisis* Letter art plaques through exhibition themes to highlight different issues or ideals to share art or display what was created either from a class or from one's own way of expression, or social art exhibit.

Shadow Kirigami as an art form has predominantly been scenery. With the Shadow Starflakes, the shadow is made from the cut Kirigami shapes that form in the center of the cut design of the Fated Starflakes layouts

Introduction to Kirigami cut Starflakes

Asian paper cutting arts in Japan known as Kirigami, the art of cutting paper along with Origami, the art of folding paper. All around the world, there are defined styles of creating arts and crafts out of cutting paper. The folding and cutting of paper in some cultures were to give spiritual reverence and used in festivals, weddings, and special occasions symbolizing luck and happiness. Today the influence of Kirigami is seen in fashion from laser cutouts in clothing, paper crafts like cutting snowflakes, even in science and technology the study of nano Kirigami for the future possibility of production of small computer parts, and chips with predictive cutting to form specific shapes on the nanoscale. Papercutting adorned religious scenery and decorative Jewish marriage contracts or prenuptial agreement also paper cutting art decorated plaques in Jewish homes placed on walls for prayer directed toward Jerusalem. In Switzerland lace-like paper cutting, in France silhouette art plaques from paper cuttings. The cultural and historical use of paper-cutting art around the world has many customs that are for spiritual reverence and praise or meditation, but also for decoration, bringing together a festive appeal, and given as gifts or exhibited artwork. Sometimes using shadows for silhouettes or casting shadow silhouettes. My hope for the Stars of Fate Starflakes, interwoven cut pieces of paper Kirigami art, and Anti-Crisis Letters are for prevention of self-harming behavior, normalize seeking help, and a way of giving support to those that just need an encouraging support system.

Shadow Kirigami as an art form has predominantly been scenery. With the Shadow Starflakes, the shadow is made from the cut Kirigami shapes that form in the center of the cut design of the Fated Starflakes layouts. Shadow Starflakes highlight mental disorders that may be hidden. Colored Vellum or other plastic paper used similar for the Paradise Starflakes theme, for problem-solving techniques.

Journal Therapy / Art Journal / Narrative Therapy

Journaling and giving accountability is a very good way to see the progression of certain life factors and see where problems may lay for examination, either from a personal perspective or a clinical setting. there are a variety of journaling technics and ways of journaling. whether you are writing journal entries or artistic expressive journaling. Artistic expression and using a narrative to highlight ideals and give perspective made from one's own words or artistic means as an approach to giving clarifying statements and ideals in an individual's life.

Giving individuals with mood disorders medications and not having a detailed journal may work for short periods of time. Long-term drug use with changes in age may be hard to determine what is adolescents or slowing metabolism, life change factors, and various risk factors from side effects of medication like headaches, nausea, vomiting, diarrhea, and other interactions. Journal entries should be detailed with physical, and cognitive data and be noted easily as possible, through cell phone calendars, journals, or art journals. Miss uses of medications, and how some diets may affect one's health. Details of time of day, diet, what was taken with the medication, what the mood of the individual was before or after taking the medication, or what day-to-day realities with the mood disorder are like. Having an outlet to express themselves may be as assessable as a phone calendar, and much easier for their phycologists or doctor to manage their health. Journaling activities and routine along with how it felt while performing a task and what behavior was exhibited or who you were with at the time with personal accountability displayed out may be good to determine choices in the future. Putting what you journal into art may help work through tough feelings and give yourself or individuals a symbol to remind you what your aspirations are. Through entries turning what was written into art or an Anti-Crisis Letter, setting goals of creativity and expression may release anxiety.

Everybody has their narrative in life or their own spin on an event and telling their own story to give meaning to life's stories and Narrative Therapy or other counseling may help give context to rationalized actions. Interactions with other individuals may help through events that may have been unavoidable and a cause of PTSD trauma.

Using The Anti-Crisis Letters or Letters of Hope and Light as a tool for a furthering approach to give more insight to help deescalate situations and are also sent from individuals to show their support through troubling times a way to connect to someone in need of help, or just encouraging words. During times of trauma or unforeseen events, the gift of kindness and knowing what others have been through and what helped them or just knowing that their part of a support system to get them the help that might be needed. The symbol of the Stars of Fate Starflakes can give the inspiration to let someone in need let them know that they are not alone.

Narrative therapy may help in certain situations when dealing with an individual narrative, writing prose in narrative imagery as part of narrative therapy conversation but trying not to have a protagonist or antagonists to seemingly blame for actions or inactions. The individual that is telling a narrative can still be the protagonist or hero of their own stories but having or trying to find a neutral perspective on individuals own may help shed light on a topic that is not easily seen.

Anti-Racism Crisis Letters

Bullying and Racist acts towards individuals may have devastating consequences, whether it's comments or actions. Singling out individuals may have just as devastating effects if wanting to show support to someone use good judgment. Being able to say in an individual's own words to give their own account is paramount in understanding and being understood; hopefully, in words and art, people can hear and be heard.

Culture awareness in symbols for pride in country and religious symbols all have a place and can have a profound effect. Using symbols for support and not harsh connotation, using art and words to heal and support may have lasting effective support structures. For the Anti-Racism Crisis letters having cultural awareness is key to be a supportive structure and with different cutting and stylistic methods of combined art forms fusing personal preference to cultural awareness, bringing together the Starflakes as a way of expression and bringing cultural awareness can take many forms.

Preface In Prose

Getting to a place that is to be how life is being lived and questioning life along the way. Being at the point to where distraction is found when having conflicting thoughts and being someone too afraid to seek help and to be asked about what actions have been unappealing. Only to be fearful of responded answers that is to be just thoughts and images in a mind of confusion. Wanting to give more of what should be given. Apprehension that is too difficult to get what must be completed and finding ways to accomplish goals of pressing importance. Being someone that should have no shame but feeling made shameful by a life that is guided by Fate, progressing to a point to where nothing is felt right. Finding that asking the same questions to seem to find answers but not wanting to talk about issues that seem forthcoming. Having given time in life to what is now to be just memories of what use to be exciting and familiar. Seeming to now be weary of actions by others and being more fearful of what is consuming from the inside.

Images of spiraling into repeated darkened holes and reaching a point to where nothing can escape, looking around to find a guiding pathway to where life was to lead. Trying to not feel cheated but feeling cheated out of a life that was so promising with change that would be ratifying and differences challenging to a lifestyle wanted. Having to find what is missing to know more about life that has passed with an unfamiliar part of life that is now left. Wanting to know but knowing I would not like to hear the answer that I would give or hear the answers that would be given. Knowing what was having to be done to keep fear from overcoming the willingness to succeed in a life that was seemingly useless but not wanting to embrace help from healing hands and falling in arms so harmful to a soul that needed comfort.

A verity of help by caring individuals but more cause for alarm from the state of numbness and no feelings from what was offered to be more harm than what was to be long term healing. Seeing what was to be help to who needed it and what help was given, with gazing of disgrace, insincere looks of sympathy, and little understanding.

Out pouring of issues to therapeutic hearts that help sort out life's and worth the time and energy spent. Some finding the way their life works and are very comfortable with what time has granted them. Some seemingly to have sunken too far into what is now reliving pain at times of what triggers downfalls. Going too far into something that could be helpful could be very hurtful or head strong with a deceptive will of an individual having to find avaricious happiness. Feeling let down by kindness and trying to help others to the point of hindrance to a life that tries to provide comfort. Having gotten helped along the way, to find that giving more than what is tolerable.

The Stars that are in us and are all around us that help guide us, to show that life is worth prices of failure, and glories of our success. Some spirited rejoicing from our interceded light may have to be pressured to truly shine. Letting our lighted path be found without trying to put what we believe to help us is not right for everyone.

Stars of Fate Starflakes

The *Stars of Fate, Starflakes* are different parts of feeling that needed to be expressed. It is something visual that can be seen, and what is felt to show others, but to most they look like snowflakes or don't look anything like snowflakes. The *Stars of Fate* started to shine from a hole that was felt in a heart that needed comfort, and moments that have been some of the toughest times, and a time of refection with release of emotions that are at times hard to explain.

#Threading Stars

#Threading Stars is a book to show different parts of feelings or emotions expressed in Narrative imagery prose poetry and show different parts of expression through crafting of *The Stars of Fate Starflakes*.

The chapters

Stars of Light are inspired paths that have been illuminating feelings that have helped healing.
Suicide Stars are actions that have led to paths that have been growing experiences.
Stars of Fait Accompli are the lighted paths that has guided and inspirited.
Ribbons of Truth are truths that have been reviled through life sometimes to be painful and some to be rewarding to see what was being felt.
Coloring the Stars is a combination of several of the Narrative Imagery prose poems and sometimes gives an understanding of what was trying to be conveyed.

The use of the word suicide in *Suicide Stars*

We do need to understand more about suicide and be aware of social issues when suicide is part of our life. Using the word suicide does weird things to people and people act differently when you use the word because it is a scary thought and when the word is brought up the imagery that it brings up is just as scary. When the dialog does come up it is usually after someone has died of suicide. The public facilities that are made to help seem not to be affective for long periods of time, or it will just take time to deal with the issues at hand for some individuals. When looking for help there are many ways to seek and when there are so many ways to go, usually it means there is seemingly no real way to help, and everyone seems to have a different theory where it comes from and how to treat it because every situation is different and can be caused by many internal and external factors.

The use of the word suicide in Suicide Stars is to define a group of emotions that come from a scary place inside, that at times seem to be counterproductive and regressing to a state of mind that helps deal with internal issues in a way of releasing emotions that are difficult to explain.

Letters of Hope and Light the *Anti-Crisis Letters*

The letters of Hope and Light the Anti-Crisis letters are letters with a Star of Fate wrapped around words to inspire and help repair, sent to let someone know that a caring thought is present trying to make a unity of helping hands. Giving an ease of thought with words of inclusion in hope of preventing a crisis from acts of fears; that leave impressions that can harm without knowing the true impact from ideas that need to be adjusted to satisfyingly calm a displeasing unrest.

Stars of Light

Letting Things Fall into Place

The followed threads can leave behind a taste of regret if not dealing with the certainly of knowing where feelings come from then being able to deal with what is left behind.

Not to discourage or shame with disgrace. To find that if feelings cannot seem to clear the lingering appeal of bitterness can set in and stay within a failing placement of self-worth.

The stars of light have followed and the dealing of placement of blame can alter perception within a lost feeling.

Having an inspirational character to show that paths that may have to be revealed to find time to let everything fall into place without a pressed conclusion.

Fractal of Light
Pieces of repeated crystalline fallen from the sky in infinite fractals of such beauty in nature, a coldness that has a sharpened grasp of chilling thoughts that confuse and then not able to sustain.

A breath being given and then taken with factored attrition to melt the amazing work away, looking for answers that could bring clarity to a waste of such precious life and kept willingness at bay.

Not able to answer questions that have waited for happiness to remain through importance. Angrily not knowing why there is no answer to have strayed from a path from remained brightness; trying to find why a fractal of light would willingly fade from a given breath to limit such a beautiful day.

Sought Fractal of Light
Doing what is felt to be right and knowing what actions to take heed when seeking for answers to bring; seeking points of light that are being made and powerless for answers, just listen to what must be said.

Having to be done and having enough courage to seek help in times of need and to respect courage to start and others will follow a fractal of light to make it more than what was ever thought could be seen.

Not only will the strengths be found but strengths that will bring courage completely profound change. Seeking out a fractal of light may just begin when thought that a light was sure to fade to just begin; seek out fractals of courage to be spread by infinite light or start what was thought to end with a fight.

Pulsing Change
Trying to live in surroundings that seem confined by a point of view that restrains true feelings; to finding irritating pain to pulse with sounds of frustration buzzing around clever minded deception.

Radiating from courage a comfort of forgiving voices to receive clear reckoning of traveled personalities; calling out for completion needing to finish the developing concept of forgiving heartbreak rationally.

Pulsing change to give a set rhythm to pace a heart to beat for a loving nature that changes personality to know that untamed wanting of accomplishments linger from indecisiveness to heed the call of destiny.

Empathetic Heart

Being lashed out at and falling laid out in fashion of such abuse; livid and well spent body that doesn't get use to inappropriate words that represent ignorant life.

Hearing the laugh of such people that represent the preponderance of mocked singular groups, tears from hearts from well lived individuals moved within by light that moved such a heart to act.

Acting with such great strength to offer a hand to who is in need, because the helping hand remembers when they were once was prostrate.

Suppression at Hand

Superstition and habit that let you feel comfort in what is destined to happen, looking at what could be if you are lucky enough to be afforded the possibility to be granted by chance.

The clash of fate and wanting to be a part of something so grand, expecting action for the hand of fate to carry you through the times that are to come; waiting on the hourglass to run out, to act on what could be altering but suppressed by a hand.

Lost Without Blame

Being led by commanding authority into fields to end up lost and knowing that mistakes are made, wanting to believe in a leader that is above just standing in a higher rank.

Needing to see that someone is not perfect to be great at navigating in darkness and seeing how being lost can show light and a sign of humanity not frailty.

Being able to find a true leader and to accept their faults with knowing mistakes happen, not wanting to be lost but needing to find out that life is learning humility without always placing blame.

Accommodated Interruption

Fantastic fiction from ideals diverged from daydreams in minds so willingly seeking love, finding loving treatment at times of exchanged banter with someone that accommodates disruption.

To find testing sanity and to bring a broken heart foolishly trying to find love with an interrupting of a search, not being fooled into something that takes on a bigger meaning than just selfish gratification.

Accommodating interrupting behavior to give loving support in times that needs repair with a wholehearted risk that might collapse an inflated head and heart from heaviness of fiction.

Strength of character tested when so much is at stake from a lovingly mistake and an interrupted fate, feelings interrupted by wildly imaginative kindness yet deprived kind touches from dear companions, not being able to modify fated timing and time needed to heal a mind interrupted by a touch.

Artful Light

The intercepting might of guidance along a destine path fulfilled by the brilliance of knowledge.

Regardless of faults of diverse cultured journeys along the way being shielded proposals of malevolence.

Totaling inspired goals to unequaled amounts of gratitude from inspirations of selfless eyes of trust.

Artful light never led astray from knowing that sacrificed comforts to having great works of kindness.

Forced Gratitude

Not given in hand with rightful belonging a serviced desire of such a willing component of greed.

To not having to force a hand in fate if just asked to get what was desired in times so disappointing in nature of forced desire.

Dealing with life as it comes but seeming to come faster than expected and not able to overtake gracious offense.

Trying not to force a hand of habit to refine a capable justice with what has taken hold so lustfully.

Odd Greatness

Is it so odd for me to expect someone so great to be with, or be it too late to expect greatness?

Having no other way but to say I do deserve the greatness I have always felt to be with deserving gratitude.

To be alongside with something great in longing eyes, to be with and be happy with at will and surprised by natural comfort.

The oddness that is to be a peculiar grandness that is an uprising to fated selected pride.

If found so willingly excepted faults that are not to be so openly denied by something so great in size.

Encompass to find a Breath

Doing for me what I could never give to you, somewhere to feel a belonging to, clueless from worry and no matter what is wrong you turn right into the directed path of ego.

Living to be an example of what makes everything seem to have beautiful revolution inside, when seeing a smiling face that makes a world seem like its ready to bloom.

To be comfortable in a skin that use to be lost from contact to where you want to swoon.

Fooling your Heart

Trying to pass on an opportunity that is not meant for you to press upon fate, seeing what is caught by just a glimpse and knowing it is not yours to take hold.

Dreams held by a heart of someone else that brings substance to soulful retreat to try to gain by deceit.

A desire of golden relief to ease pain that seems to be long-lasting to want to tip scales of favored existence.

An aspiring soul fitting in a world you feel you were not meant to belong but seeing yourself walking in.

Realizing that you do belong to a brilliance you have come to fit in your life but still unwilling to share to only be fooling your heart.

No Word

No words have been exchanged for a bit, I should not have to apologize, I'm sorry to admit.

I still have love for you, and all around the love for all, relative feelings have run their course, and it may be hard to be around at all.

For my thoughts very, and verifying thoughts of me, I know it does not have to be said nor need explanations to be spoken.

Love for me it will always be, but trust for all it is hard to say, I have no word to express how I feel, and no clue how to express my feelings for you.

More of the Same

More of the same, and not at all what were thought to be truths to be exacting promises, love for most, but not for anyone that can be found so lovingly fond of a broken heart.

Losing that made many sorrowful to find that there was more to find from listening; hollowed out hearts that have faded into paths that are not relevant in life's direction.

There is so much to be done in lives that have more to show than twisted reality, yet nothing can be done to reason with others, who still are filled with hate toward losing.

How do you find a path that is not your own and can it be the right fit for someone so reluctant?

Others filing their loss and taking part of life's dissimilar and distant from where life was heading, to found paths that has no bearing and intentions being the same but with detoured directed life.

Pacified by Suspicion

A mouth shut by suspicion that can only lead to conclusions indiscernible through encrypted meanings, wanting to know more but stumbling by confusion being brought to hearts dreadful deductions.

Having to know that what the easiest understanding to be the truth that betrayal has forced awareness, to find that a simple test of truth to be more indulgent than the lies being told to confuse.

Trust

All I want to know are feelings of what has already happened but not talked about, secrets that are buried but everyone seems to know about, it's easy for some to lie and have been taught how to not tell the truth, and not to show how you feel.

Our heads have been held high and love has never been held back yet seeing the cost hearts have paid to keep some feelings buried deep inside so hidden from each other.

Living life in extraordinary pain and guilt laid on weighted lives but not living the life you wanted to live and not able to deeply trust complete.

To Start a New

A new beginning in steps we take each day to start a new, from the beginning of an ended road.

A new self is in each step we take to better the beautiful place we call our own, the places that are our home.

We can shine from the inside out and let the outside shine bright, we just must find our own light and find use in the steps we take to start a new.

A Themed Cause

Not understanding why life is working out to be themed by no reasonable answer; reasons found for leaving that have no comfortable way of expressing reasons for staying.

Eyes of mistrust in themed motives of horror with anger displaced willingly; unexpected way of living to form healing bonds so keen to progress reminiscently. The themed cycle of what life must be or what life is becoming and reasons that will show in time.

You are Mine; I am Yours

Throughout life we go being called all names to try to define us, some good some not, some to raise us up, or bring us down. At the end of the day those who love us, know who we are, and you know who they are, they accept us no matter who calls us by whatever name, they believe in us no matter what we are called.

No one knows where life will lead them, and when life will bring them down. When you find someone that loves you no matter what you are called is when life begins; life is beginning for me for you are mine and I am yours.

Resolution

Health, wealth, and wisdom people seek, resolute to dissolve issues that bring misery to the meek.

Wanting more for people's lives that have a lot at stake, captivate all who see your seceding light; resolutions of selfless honor in actions to meet, having a resolution of living life with no regrets to make.

Corruptive Distance

Influenced under pressure that brings untrustworthy activity to mind when distanced in possibilities, looking for more than an escape from disparaged quality of life in burdening jealousy.

To finding a troubling fight in a world of crushing cruel spirited frustrating situations. Going about with a hand alongside a disdained character to encouraged senseless acts of infidelity; showing nothing being forgiven if not willing to progress and trust without a trusting behavior.

Lost in Your Touch

You've wondered what I have thought so I will tell you in my own way, you make me think of ways to care, you make me laugh with a touch, you make me shiver when I am hot, you make me lose my thought, and then I lose my place. You make me feel you truly care; you make me smile because I see what a great person you are.

The thoughts go wild in my head, but I must admit I am a bit deceiving, and a smile can mean many things, sometimes I'm not sure myself, and some smiles are my secret I keep.

Falling Stars

Constellations of the Stars that are surrounding us, being so close yet can't touch us, falling from clouded thought that confine screams of the stars that are not heard.

Many never acknowledged that are around us that seem so distant but saw so close to us, so many emotions that breath is feeling wasted, and time is only antagonizing.

Disappointed at life and agony that does not subside, never known by willingness to hide, falling stars are all around us and cries surround us, not listened to, or ignored by sealed ears by all of us; needing hope from delightful life to offer hope that could be anyone of us.

Stepped Into Finality

Signaled frequency highlighted every beat of an end that can only encourage defeat, reduced to negotiable acceptance of coursed incorporated soulful performed sound.

Growing interest to rework an enthusiastic release of melody to entranced simplicity, stepping into a beat of torment of a life so simple to give a debut of selfless courage.

Attempts of enjoying a nonstop melodic symphony of atmospheric sounds of integrity, electronic loyalty of infamous sounds of technology to be discarded territory of culture.

Final scratched beats of perfection to be heard repeated randomly selected ferocity.

Winds of Opinion

People coming in and out of your life for reasons unknown, through difficult times life lessons to learn, giving and given opinions and taking away knowledge from who we meet.

Ranging from friends that make you happiest when they express themselves, to critical people that twist facts that ring no bells of truth.

Your own remembered self-image of what had been so promising and where life is leading, opinions that have various weights in your life, taking what's needed and sharing lives with love.

Seeing yourself from different points of light that makes real the chosen routs that have been taken, all brings radiance of opinion to your life to find what has been with you just not seen.

Moving on with your life at your own pace and not getting caught up in the bad images of life, long lines of pain that run through and must be dealt with, to not destroy a future so bright.

Sorting through the images to find what has been false and what has been so true even by critical light.

To not getting caught up in negative points of opinion that may stain with time, links of love and life's friends bring happiness and winds to push you through the roughest of opinions.

Restless Craze

Thoughts of sorrow with no need to explain if no understanding is going to be found; wondering how things can begin when seemingly not able to start to look forward.

Restless anxiety from a detailed day with awkward thoughts for problems to solve, dreaming haze of delusion from the storm in your head but seeing the calm all around.

Thought of Touch

A glimpse of what could be from a chance encounter, the want of an embrace that feels so strong but makes you weak; a hope to embrace that is to be returned and amazed by what you are sharing.

Thoughts of what may come and only to be lost in ideals in your head, to be lost in thoughts that are just images that can't seem to be expressed.

So many thoughts but no words being said, feelings being lost with no words to impress said, a show of expression, a wishing you could express, and an ideal that brings a glimmer to an imagination with just a thought of a touch.

Turbid Thoughts Confusing

In a mind so overcome by what is only in thoughts that have anxiety of fearful rescue, not wanted to be saved from a place that offers more than what would be taken away.

Muddleheaded by what is supposed to be so freeing to lose so much, to have turbid thoughts of confusion to waste the moment with jealousy.

Turgidity of feelings in a (Heart so Weakened)

Verbose and repeated complements that mean nothing when not heartfelt, when so much is said how do you reply to something that makes no sense?

No use trying to explain when nothing is wanted to be heard, and what is said dismissed, when explanations make less common sense than what foolish behavior is presented.

Thoughtful Purchase

Giving into helping hands to let forgiveness come gradually when processing thought to provoke change, knowing what's best to not give in willingly when no ability to see effects of change immediately.

Trying to be more pleasant to embark on a forgiving pathway into dealing with past pursuits honestly; reality sets in on sun striking days that needs to let freedoms straddle hopeful journeys purchasing a life's pathway.

Veil

In a shroud of something that is hard to make since when found so confusing, words that have no meaning and you have no understanding of context.

People that have no reason for being in a life that is so deceiving, feeling alone in rooms that are filled with life and nothing being spoken with true understanding.

Coming to find that more life being lost in disbelief from what is so evident, finding no reason for being in places that are disabling.

Not sure why it's difficult to be yourself and knowing you're coming off as fake, touches of some are chilling, too cold to take, and being lost with someone so conceded is too much to take.

Giving into remarks that make lies so easy to believe and passed off as fate, to find that what you see, and feel are being concealed and lost in a mind covered in hate.

Knowing the answers to questions, but too risky to be revealed and too hard to take; lifting a veil of confusion to see what has always been so true and your life can be easier to give when raising a veil to see your true fate.

A Lighted Gift

Expressions of what you feel and come from your heart to your hand, with detail that brings depth and color to strokes to make objects come alive with design.

Two perfect shapes that make perfection of such modern design; an ideal that takes shape of perfect design with gifts able to pass to granted lighted presence. A gift to have such perfection just needing to realize a talent before it seems to be lost as easily as it came.

Dawned a True Day

Living in compromise and sacrifices made that have a cost, no true feelings expressed and needing to release of frustrated thought.

Being grateful for what has been done and given love that could do no wrong, blocked off and hidden life to conceal feelings that were never to be turned into words.

A wall that took so long to build to now feel like everything that was to be true to be gone.

Close to Failure

Finding things that are truly specific and with great taste and people that have attitudes the same, when Life is so shocking and when you need someone to be on board of something that is to come.

Never letting regret being able to win when you have found a friend and not letting failure repeat, having to look for what is seemed to be lost and to never letting life pause for what could be a defeat.

Long Road

Words of encouragement that keep you on track to let you know that you are a piece of shared life, caring thoughts to be known from living alongside together given inspiration of future roads.

Having let the other steer at times to keep you on track to travel back toward the right path, inspired guide to you with a directed life so you would not lose your way even though the other is lost.

Condoned Activity

Condemned from activity that was a surprising destruction of condoned conformity, acts of violence are chosen at times of imperiling danger to end with no victor and loss of importance.

Frightened line of unity to verge through a faulted issued alliance between constructed dominance was not a choice but is now a breach of confidence that trust will have to be received at a higher cost.

Fresh Balance

Some that never can see what is in front of faces and do what is needed, misunderstood, and set into jokes and not given a chance to let a light show what is to be given.

Needing to be level in thoughts and actions to give what is needed from your life; to give a heart that cannot bear disappointment balance in lives journey to share. Treasured people that need you to be in lives that are far from where your path was leading.

Feeling Change

Letting actions not to determine who you know you can be from a standing you are now forgiving, being present in the state of mind you are in to be a gift you can give if given a chance.

Letting yourself feel and be who you have intended to be without changing uniqueness, not turning into an imposture so what you feel to be given is fresh guidance.

Concerned about the intended change for the need of progression and feeling lost in satisfaction, being present in the state of mind you are found in no matter what situation you are in.

Living Magnanimous

Getting so much more from giving yourself to such a cause to go into action, calling on past light to give guided paths a hopeful future to more than what seems to be given.

A magnificent life and prosperous virtue in this grand being to be more than just a saying. Brought by such an outstretched time that does not limit the nature of giving souls; the fortitude of dreams that is still prevalent for a life that can give so much when living with gifts so generous.

A True Heart

Brightness being brought to your heart with such an exhilaration to a life so plain, but a heart so true, definite in a direction to have made a path with love bestowed with willingness of being pursued.

Now to be misleading of a distinct road and missing a loving brightness that you were so sure, finding their path was not so defined to have in common that you hoped to pursue.

Letting go to let trueness be given in other ways of living without giving into a disaster matching rivalry, to a life so plain and a heart so true, a   love that cannot be taken hold and having to relinquish control.

Leaving with Adoration

The sea of ever going peace to come to try the will of determined adoration, to find the roads are full, but the air is freeing to a dependent association with consuming addiction.

To not throw an unwilling being into a hole of guilt, gluttony, or grievous killing of pain, knowing you're not the best, but doing the best is not what you have been found to be best at.

With flash frames of darkness and life passing by, bettering through a change may be worth trying; a battle to win, a life to live, and a road to take to put yourself into power to change your life.

Needing to find what is wanted and worth giving up, to what is worth keeping from destruction.

Strength Of light

Patience being short, and life wanting to be lived in comfort of light, a once bitter fusion of a heart that had been threatened to be turned to stone not knowing if able to work through past to ever feel a truly belonging.

Hearing the storm in your head but seeing the calmness all around to give a hand to strengthen a weakened self-image you have found.

Being embraced by something so big that consumes your life when you're not the strongest; all strength of will to have illuminated kindness to break the taste of bitterness.

Following Your Path

Traveling the way that is felt right, pursued destiny with revealed light along the way, thinking you know but not knowing how to start, to begin by just taking the first step.

Not wanting to hurt to be a risk but a risk worth the rewards if you're willing to take; needing to know that your life is not defined by a lustful light and what is at stake; with remembering your heart is a star shined bright with the presence of insight and delight.

Caring Souls Beginning

A life meaning well with a loving mind and a caring soul, not sure what has been asked but willing to go, mindful of people and caring acts to some with nothing more wanted but a kind greeting to show.

There is no way to know how people feel until you ask and not knowing can be easier to ignore; taking time to tell some how you feel may help end a route to what may be a beginning for you.

Lifetimes of Memories

Short moments of interest with time pressing on and truths grown deep, changing urges from day to fade into passing feelings from what you say.

Living up to potential of what thoughts belong with passing age, encouraging words to pull you through hostilities to leave you with a lifetime of memories.

Come to find it takes what should come so easy to say and be so grateful to fulfill; a lifetime of moments that need to be felt in detail.

Situations of Unrest

Protective light surrounding and unknown actions that keep prevailing, minutes that could have changed events and fateful accidents that have reasons for existing.

Unknown hazards stopping from traveling down paths not kept prevailing love to seek caring light to embraced with true fit to inspired darken soul to commit.

Lost in Thought

A wish you couldn't express and brightness of light that is beaming but never taking time to display, diminishing the darkness that you thought would be forever expressed in thoughts not so easy to forget.

A longing to share life and wanting to show a true self that was never possible to give without dread, finding a true coupling in impossible friendships that have all led to the same ending to start recycling.

Hoping to find that openness is still worth trying to not let fear get the best of life's worthy of forgiving, getting lost in thoughts to let go of regrets of what should have been to live in dream-built possibilities.

Exonerated Beastly Expression

Giving out what was so hard to take by such harshness of expressed dislike of adoring character, ailing thoughts that converge in weakness and unease in mind and soulful body exhaustion.

After thoughts that flow through mind numbing inability to pursue a clearing process. Heartaches from loss that time needs sweetness in life to be given with sweat laden body from toil; making life ready for love that may come to cool an overheated manor of beastly expression.

Difficult to Find

Finding a cause that makes sense to give your time to end wasting precious motivation when needed, some comfort from knowing but hardly worth trying when feeling defeated by disruption.

Given strength to causes to be taken at a disadvantage of falling behind a presumed future in failure, starting to find that it's difficult to have time to dwell in past to find perspective.

Harder to believe in time being taken to find the end when looking for the beginning, living closer to feared missed opportunity than wanting to admit a harmful subject is present.

Justice to know what is clear, it's just difficult to find when looking for a substitute when lost in time, outlined path to give a hand in found difficulty to let go to have room to grow from what was misplaced.

Destine To Change

Can you change your destiny, and can things be destined to fail, what if you think you're changing but just doing the same thing?

Is it wrong to try to get something or someone if you know that it's going to fail, or is it holding you back from something great? What is worth losing to get the life you want, would losing yourself be enough?

Is it change or progression that makes you question the progression of changing life, is it worth the daredevil dream or was it ever meant to be questioned?

Companions So Right

Beauty so bright that flows with grace with all the music that fills hearts throughout the night. Smiles that beam with joy and tearful eyes that are with such happiness that has been given delight; union with a lifelong search of fusion that makes lives fill with light from companions that feel so right.

Words on Paper

Overwhelming words of such length built up through time and following you were ever you have gone; kindness past and cruelness remembered from words that have shown no surrender.

More therapy in content than inspiring views to have been written with no need to choose. Words have traveled through the years with memories intact and actions remembered; words to have now been written down to remember and not delivered, just pen strokes on paper.

Natures Hand

Weather sweeping in unseen harmful lengths undetermined time of circumstance, needing caring souls that take care into their hands being guardians placed in times of need.

Detouring with diversions needed to avoid dangers on paths that where to be crossed. Guidance that is nature leaving a lingering touch of expressed need of urgent delay; natures hands that grasp control to show what was misplaced to gain ground in giving space to let nature have its way.

Hart's Star

A star that was so binding to friends that have now parted ways, in different compartments of family and friends his star lit dark paths.

Not ashamed of acts that were so boldly kind and not willing to give less than his best. A remarkable star that gave so much but had other plans that weren't on display; remarkable life that marks such destruction of celebration of his Independence Day.

Tearing Down to be Built Up

A desired design of a dilapidated structure that needs repair with considered revising in construction, needing more than the ability to be taken care of with the insecurity of being so reasonably torn.

A start of destructiveness that needs loving hands to care for the known dysfunction that is hopeless consumption of praiseworthy functions.

As an independent structure with need of a foundation to be set in understanding but knowing inability of controlling activities.

Structures of personalities that can be rebuilt but needing to be satisfied with the process unfolding; building a new aesthetically pleasing character with sensible living and built understanding of giving.

Slowly Moving Inward

Slow moving character but quick to retreat if having to change from loving exaggeration of confusion, reacting from a charge of self-denial to having to quickly defend and trying to preserve selflessness. Savoring time given when having feelings that cover calmness with an anxious vulnerability to kindness.

An importance to strength of inner worth from peaceful return to knowledge to not doling judgment; no use trying to absorb an experience if drifting thoughts tear facts from faulty perceptions.

Way of Mischief

Two hearts that are a perfect fit with a design that stands in place to comfort a way of mischief, looking as if it has always been set in place.

Calming and beautifully conjoined to show a practical belief. Worlds that have ways of mischief in colorful lives that has more past to connect and future to shine; something in-between that binds beauty tightly with connections to catch such beauties site with intrigued delight.

Nomadic Hearts

Roving about to find what is missing to find traveling farther than wanted to find a perfect match in your position, taking steps to show fluid movements from place to place to not show past heartaches. To find waking with a taste of mistrust for souls forsaken by lies that has taken tolls on lives.

Can moving on just be taken by hand to forget or forgive yourself for being so open, forgiving to love to live and find a place to move onto without regression or taken steps to possession of what was misplaced with misfortune.

Constructed Life

With plans that have brought such passion and truths to be caught by hearts that feel exact, having constructed a life without the need to show each other what has gave them their identity.

To show what is important to be hidden, not seeing what is to be given and not knowing what to give when not knowing what to ask.

Finding that you have more to give and less to take when you feel empty with no connection, lives still being constructed and anticipation of building together but built farther than what is certain.

Waves of Life

Water makes peace but waves can find and pass right through or demolish at times; life can be calm and peaceful or seemingly be tough to go through and impart silence.

Waves that crash against you to seem to never subside and life will prevail and find a course to extend, waves of change to find breaks and stalls in living to knock you off balance to keep you focused.

Goals at hand to overcome to have peace that passes through so you can make waves of change.

Stars Inside

Stars inside and not afraid to show through a rough exterior with essence of fervor, feelings that are not wanted to be felt, but hesitant to feel happiness. Stars that shine brightly to burn, and too sharp to cut deep from with-in.

Betrayal and jealousy that cannot be explained, from actions that seem uncontrolled, not accepted in a life that is being lived and love that is being had.

Loved ones that could never know the person that is part of life that is now feeling complete. Not ashamed and no need to conceal, just not knowing how deep the betrayal lie; if so brightly lit and light is seen, why are the stars that are trying to show so hard to share.

Defending an Ego

Being pushed into a complicated scenario to have to defend respect by presenting a false image, not wanting to concede to a demanding failure and cannot admit defeat when defending an ego.

Confidence betrayed from embarrassing situations that seem to course inflamed temper rapidly, not wanting to go to a place of harmful action but not wanting to display cowardly affection.

Tapping into an extreme feeling that makes for a poor decision to start with obstinacy; an embarrassing show in a situation that is hard to control with harmful advisements in tow.

Feather Light

Feather lightly through movement entranced beauty of points of airy breath giving life to stars that would be still and added silhouette of elegance in back lit shadows.

Outstanding possibilities that let who need to look up to something positive in a dimly lit world. Giving softness to a hard-edged form, feathery dusting of cascading comfort down isles of thorns; treed though the night with wings of grace to give peace to who needs to be consoled in a soft light.

Flood of Emotions

Remembering how life has changed and how easily memories slip away to not expect ration to betray, surprising what memories come back in such extreme ways, to now be forced to come to terms.

Overwhelmed by what has come to be, to inure what seems to be a strengthened presence bestowed, endured what was thought to be fatefully giving what you could modestly and giving in earnestly.

Making the most of the flood that could come to be if you are to accept in a promise so complete.

Midnight Consumption

Having more to contribute than giving into reasons for a disposable accompanied friendship, looking for more than midnight pleasure to fulfill a delectable craving of luscious giving.

Flourishing in life with reasonable taking of nourishing resources to promote suitable morals, going to lengthy routines made for selfish use of disgusting habits to indulge ravenous behaviors.

Fared well in a graded limit to need more in life than wild consumption of late-night compassion, wanting to have a companion lighted union to bring levels of insecurity outspoken in diversity.

Dynamic Feedback

Synthesized in rhythm paradise becoming enclosed in breaks in beating hearts, compositions of collections that fills walls to vibration weigh feelings uninterrupted by discomfort of crowded imposition.

Mood of energetic rhythm flowing through with movement of exaggeration, feeling at home to discover artistic light blinding you in dynamic feedback.

Threaded Stars

Threaded in light and giving more effort of an underestimated desire to succeed, yet not dealing with the situation of irritable shining words of tolerance from what seems to be judgment.

Even if an escape into an unknown state of comfort can be dealt with in a miscalculation of way of innocence, can it still be just. Not letting the comfort of acceptance be blinding to your perception from a claim of rightful authority. Processes that can keep you from beginning and not letting the systems of absorbed stress be put in place of your found identity. Threading each star to its place of greatness and being put in awkward standings of complacency if not getting the correct care of helpful reserved time of consistency.

Settling in Austerity

Sun set starkness not being noteworthy to have disciplined accountability to form structure, in what is to be a life having to deal with what is left from willingness to live a plain life yet fulfilling. Seeing life in posterity and having the inability to have the use of what is now simplicity. Knowing what is to be given up having a change of accommodations that are a far gaze of past luxury.

Moment to Clear

Affectionate essence of arousing individual spirited movement to find tender clarity, letting go of vulgarity and being pensive about relations of maturity.

Comfort in places to unite and have use for upholding peaceful integrity, being graceful and showing situations unraveling to indicate solidarity.

Working Through

Going through issues of mistrust and thinking you are above the situation of distrust, coming to the realization that being found to have the same issues and being in frustration.

Feeling worthless and finding no solution that is workable from a point of damaged participation, trying to find easier routes to find that you can't seem to get passed issues with no complaint.

Justification to hold accountable of regression causing contributing disbelief, releasing burdens to stop harboring counted traumatic falls from standing in unworkable situations.

Not Accepting Brutality

Only giving what is seen in a nightmare of shaded personality to be given marked strength. Life that is worthy of love but finding to negotiate with point mindedness with unfair advantages, being griped by the inability to stray from commitment and finding acceptance in generosity.

Finding what was given to be received in brutality and accepting that change is considered with growing. Not defined by confined condemning circumstance in brutal nature of childhood disturbances, just not being able to give up tendencies as easily as wanted and finding help is needed will be received.

Historic Stars of Light

Past thoughts that have more pain than playful innocents, brought about thoughts of anger but now seem to have no relevance.

Looking back through thoughts that have points of interest. Living and actions that bring memories that have yet to fade; paying honor to past and knowing what past is still present in the light of day.

Years to Be

Greetings that pass and evil that is presented so beautifully to keen eyes of integrity, bigger parts of life that brings love when needed to shine when feelings are being tested. Harmful attitudes that try to take what was worked for so proudly through years that comes so hastily.

Years going along with joyful laughs and fun in unexpected ways that lets lives settle calmly, light that shown so bright that even makes evil dim its lights from coming to surface so readily.

Remarkably Made

With hands made something so thoughtful and given gifts of life's remarkable, something so poetically enchanted and feelings being visual that says what could not be spoken.

With hands so talented and made so caring from actions that are unmistakable, with respectful guidance from intervening light to be given to hands so thankful.

Night In

A night that is not needed to be spent rushing and smiling at people never to be seen again, with intriguing conversations that would not be started to end in disappointment.

A break from confusing relations to be spent with no one that needs explaining, a self-comforting in selfless return to image preferred point of view with no impressed components. Finding what is wanted to save from being defaced and being relaxed in complete confidence.

Seeking a Sanctuary

Refuge from distressed desolation of restless silence in wondering thoughts of instilled fortitude, not able to share the endless noise in thoughts and repeat of harbored fire of insults.

Trying to protect from bleeding hearts that are seeking trust to have an advantaged position, costly mistakes that led to a more protective state of solace and instilled coldness from negative attention.

Day of Sharing Love

Chosen day to express love's accompaniment with shared feelings of excitement, pursuit of a heart in need to give messages and tokens to keep a loving memory complete.

Given two hearts the secure wholeness of love to share though out the rest of the day with messages of sweet affection to find an unknown spark that needs to be set ablaze.

Helped Hands of Generosity

Needing helping hands that are cooperative if true acceptance is going to be granted, finding being more tolerated to not offend an accepted praiseworthy love if willing to mend.

Needing much more to be given to give a helping hand if able generous propensity is to extend, feeling true acceptance is granted and defined as worthy of a chance to extend a hand.

Persistent Struggle

Drown by corruptive opportunity in an accidental meeting thought to be a gamble worth trying, to be pressed into actives that are an accidental tragedy to be misled and now struggling to depart.

Seemingly willing to let life become a struggle to have to be pulled away by destiny but kept in captivity.

Needing to keep going on with plans that will be an endeavor worth the effort if able to escape, to get out of a desperate situation with what help can be given when being buried by acts of deception.

Luminous Separation

Many ways to turn to seem to have no solution to conflicts with frivolous explanations; finding many with goals of similar nature to bring defeat in separation of spirited needs, divided and seeming to have one purpose to find various deviations from simple beginnings.

Obscurely turned into redundancy from steps made lifetimes before to find relevance everlasting; light that progresses life to fine pints of separation to finding many points of opinion repeatedly.

Rebalanced

Being true to what is needed and wanting substance to bring simple joy from stability, keeping relevant in a life of preservation to revel in spirited joyous occasions.

Hopeful hearts that need clear skies but not for selfish gratification to balance life's altercations, self-satisfied in owning faults to make corrections to wronged situations.

Standing

Onward to find footing from outstanding obstacles that takes time to conquer, trying to find time to sit and knowing that it isn't rare to fall from position.

Life spilling over into lives that can help from slipping to what has hindered in the past, no distance that is too far to walk but finding satisfaction to stand so proudly in place.

Leading Brightness

Wanting to see a leading way that is better felt from achievement with less deceptive involvement, scared and scarred to see what life is without a sanctuary from lustful acts of indulgent comportment.

Some of the light present and fear being prevalent with unneeded argument with discouragement; insight and light farthest from sight still leads with the brightest of lights through darkest of moments.

Escaping darkness

Impossibilities that are made of fears so undeniable and letting darkness succeed, a heart that needs healing and what thoughts so undecided to be brought transparency.

Such helplessness that made imperfections relevant to find faults crippling with disappointment, heart rendering to strong disturbances that can be cleansing when expressing true emotions so freely; having content that is important to expectations of found happiness was to be so pleasing.

Beauty in Bloom

Fading into lightness of color and brightness is still in bloom from a flower that still has more to prove.

Accepted life and being adjusted to what life has to offer from what has blossomed from the coldness, succeeding to be a bright example of what can be for not given up through lengthy darkened days.

Never accepting darkness in paths that seem to loom after a frightening test of willingness to bloom, flourished through what has been a fight and still proudly standing and not in dooming decline.

Legion Queen

Sharpened points of view that taint the health of a meaningful body with needless interruption, objects of appeal that enrage conflicts of destroying autonomy and taking control of perception.

Searching for an alliance to grasp hold of control to imprison service with nothing more than promises, nothing out from a reach of a deceptive admired leading show of authority to rudely gather groupings.

Wanting the pledge of fidelity to bring about convincing darkness into a lighted authority, nothing can be given if not ready to be exploited and never too much to take when offerings of spoilage.

Expressions of Stars Hold

Harmony that is filling to stars that are unified and separating from reality, sometimes feelings that can't be hidden comes to surface that cannot offer privacy.

Realizing that expression in a callous world can lead to discouragement of passions that are being pursued, holding on to what makes beauty so easily had to not let a false form of what makes you delightful.

Needed Companionship

Being suited through times of adversity in companionship with an enduring match of witted intensity, encouraged by divine smells of fragrant love and situations of seduction that brings delight.

Brought friends to heights of love that had been amidst from sight of friendly accompaniment, endearing actions that were to necessitate hearts that were in such panic of strained existence.

Worked for goals that were set and letting go of regrets of past to solve burning issues clearly marked for companionship.

Crest of a Hopeful Discovery

Having on an armor to show humility in hopeful prevailing of certainty in discovery of esteem, turning what had made a life of misery in a body that seemed weak to a brave strength.

A controlling doubt that needs to be pierced by hope being brought through bravery, protecting the knowledge of found discovery to pass with care onto the next authority.

Pride with brave acts of certainty to have positive gains of happiness if able to remove covering of pain, to reveal the nature of deception and clarify the voices that seems to crowd thoughtful resolution.

With the crest of faith in a hopeful recovery to bring the makings of a life in greatness and gratitude, to become the shining star of revealed true brightness that gives prosperity with precision.

Shielded with bravery to command attention in hopeful plating in steal like preservation, letting fears of turmoil to rebound from decisions that were thought to bring about downfalls.

A crest of hopeful discovery to retrieve credit that is due in a life that is remarkably truly giving.

Beats so Daring

In fine tune of beats so daring finding dawning of relief in beats so striking, arriving in images of intelligent sound, mind freeing laughter consuming.

Loving smiles brightly escaping from souls so tormenting from moods so bounding. Giving generations segments of lights so inspiring; calming control to breach walls of resonance fulfilling to beats so daring.

Rock of Luck

Luck having no say to determine what is felt so possible in life of love responsible, having so much to give not to leave up to chance and to be given seconds instead of years of favor.

Luck in guessing what is to come or what has been an opportunity of great desire, chance playing a part or have feelings being granted from relief of what would be so troubling.

If found to be just a charm that gave you so much that was your choosing to leave a rock so standing.

Finding a Life

Feeling life crying out for a start of something to shadow the sadness and lifeless existence, having felt the wear of life that has not been happiness and needing more than what is being useful.

Wanting dreams to be given a chance without ridicule to find what's missing from a life of resistance, taking back your consignment to form a driven life to let attrition be a natural part of a destine course.

Misleading

Wrong direction from where you wanted to be guided that seems to have doubted steps taken, the path closer to what is wanted to find farther back than what is willing to be spoken.

Stability wanted but opposing thought prevailing to be headed too far in the wrong direction, living dangerously in steps and not sure if pausing is possible when hast in responsive character action.

When life being on hold isn't responsible and darkness has held onto hearts essence chosen selection.

Birth of Stars from a Darkened Sky

After a star has subsided the light is shown in unassuming ways to still lead down darkened pathways, housing darkness so overcoming to be taken in unwanted fears to have taken a star's light.

Wishes that were not known to be asked to be given more time to be seen from out of sight to never to be seen in the light of a star brightened night.

No comfort from loss and nothing being the same from aspect from sight when gazing at night.

Demeaning Lies

Degraded dreams by others are a risk that may come to have dreams flicker from unkind actions.

Remembering not to get caught by the deceit of unkind souls from lies being told, falling for words that have no importance in what is to come from a persistence of unpleasantness.

Being more than what is being heard and knowing what to believe when in doubt of abilities, beautiful dreams come from soul searched prisons that contribute to actions restricted by lies in a demeaning position.

Tree Height

Worries that are branching to heights that can only be seen and not able to reach. Lies adding up to more than manageable and reaching out to shade the truth, spiny things that turn and fold over and coming to points of power that need to be kept in check.

Hiding truths that could give answers to why troubles are so strangling to growth, many more things given to take out the sting of horror in perverse occasions to clear matters. Holdings that need acceptance and your own worth in high regard to not let lies be overbearing, to not take root with cumbersome deceptions that hold back truth that could give such light.

Traditions Holden by Hearts so Giving

Being honored in cultures so upstanding having love and graciousness being given. Culture rich in traditions and tightly woven into society not known for forgiving, a community that needs a loving virtue of past honored heritage to lift relations to a purposeful living. Wanting to have a merge of diplomatic trust and given fare trade to respectful upholding, for support of whom that have built a world of culture on trustful bargaining.

To now be laying claim on a life that is trying to be renewed diplomacy to nations with no treaty, being accustomed to a life that offers less than suitable surroundings to comfort in living.

Passing on comfort to be placed in darkness to progress the culture you hold so dear by abandoning.

Dodging Walls

Tunnel of imagined air propelled guidance with direction being blocked by stubborn behavior, seeing dangerous walls, and trying to doge but finding impossible to divert thought.

Various directions from underneath to over but unswerving to go right through, knowing that an easy path is from side to side but finding trying to bust right though.

To find starting from the beginning and learning as you go but losing with each pass when starting new, flying a circle to finish where you started and trying to doge a wounding wall to a path that you started.

Discrete Words of Cruelty

Safely presented by people that makes them seem unapproachable by means so thoughtful, nothing proceeded by acts just attacking discretely by talking freely justified.

Slight at hand in demeaning actions terrifying in thought to give a thrill unbecoming, matched wittiness with defense by numbness from inaction to not give rise to the vocal cruelty.

To defeat with not wasting words that can be used to rebuild a structure worth defending.

Debated Closeness

Being kept away from what can be tangible and not being fearful by what has been taken by thoughtless hands responsible.

Not given the time to make peace with a day of fearful light and not given a hope to stretch, to feel closeness to a heart from not leaving with a scorned account of lengthy debate.

To give release to issues that can be cause for actions that need to be explained with tenderness, far from a touch of calmness that can be hard to feel when nothing is felt right by words being said by those who are to be the closest.

Path to Follow

A forceful way to have beaten a path from following to now leading with great desire, to bring what is needed and not what will slow down a hurried traveler.

Going about a journey to have followed with missteps and falls to have learned measured failure, led by polished steps alongside greatness and to have helped shape the path to follow.

No matter what the traveler must overcome to end with fulfilled happiness from a path that was made alongside the fellow traveler.

Restless Triumph

Restless thought that gives no time for what is sought in anxiety; unresolved pity that gives into what is so easy to sink into.

Victory that is only for owning worth to have so foolishly despaired in times of panic, knowing that what is going to be given to have to be taken with no restraint.

From a heartless soul to a triumph that is only part of a victory in life that is worth the effort.

Masterful Delivery

Not filling up to the task of working through issues of worth, decidedly leaving in good standing to have had a skillfully mastered exit, to give life an unfamiliar context.

Demanded settled life to resist urges to give into conventional means of instruction, still unpleasant toward groupings that are current to hold position of relevance.

To now being able to give what was meant to belong to divisional life phrased text in support of feelings delivered.

Psychedelic Rhythm Planet

Here in space filled with bursting stars in unison driven out by pressure withheld all tension, souls to be set free to influence all that have seen   the stars coming from what was not to be.

A fusion of percussion punched sound out into the room of plastic kisses from electric love; smooth shock to systems unparallel   encompasses Influential tempo quality. Resonate without any comfort to be in heads filled with only hate.

Imitating the developing sounds of drums to loving mix of soul shinning youth in guidance of life, nominally swung wildly in a legendary famous blend of compositions that makes reverb furious.

Out from the sun into the night lasting until the moment seems right to leave with grand exit. From orbit in space withheld a planet of rhythm considering frightened love.

Hopeful Concinnity

Wanting so much to have a needed work of splendor to provide worth to needful surrender, a work of endeared treasure to give in willingly to a continued forgiving nature of accepting.

A gladly consuming assumption of a noteworthy character and needing relief of pressure, giving all to free sorrows released in a careful patterned behavior to inspire hopeful parts of identity.

An uncertainty to have such a wish of greatness to give into pride of a work of pain staking giving, with not giving into the comments that can harm with needless provoking of attitudes of humor, poking fun at and making a joke to laugh in no needed giving of leverage to a pest in a joking manor.

(...)

Suicide Stars

Beautiful Binding Things Within

Desperately choosing to lose a battle of importance and giving into a tempting of fate to have a need to know that if falling fast can make a desperate appeal evident.

Knowing that it may be a fight that can last with a default setting of pain when pressured and kept from expression of feelings that can be difficult to explain.

Actions that can be stopped with a choice to act on growing experiences to become a blindingly beautiful insight of life to bind together searches for something more than what is seen.

Twisted Starflakes

Metal working its way through itself with razor like edges like glass with pleasing appeal, reflected in unassuming shapes looking like it has always been one piece.

Twisted metal and sharpness of believed doubt cutting with ease, difficult feelings and unworkable detail makes life worth the work to put in effort to please. Feeling of something that may never come to pass, wanting to work with what is given, not knowing the problems that are assured to come pose doubt; Insecurity working its way through yourself with precise gaze with oddly pleasing appeal, reflected in unassuming shapes looking like you have always been one piece.

Almost

Blessings those days have shown, fears that confuse, and life that has led had been very dreary, being bitter and shy has filled and caused tears and sadness; a light has guided, from it all has made.

Troubled life to live at times has led close to almost had been to an end of the most precious gift, some words have been nothing, but hurt yet feeling sorry that if ever hurt from being led to almost.

Living in Shadows

A light that is dimming that has more to give than what is asked to share of a mind so pressed, a life that has succeeded in darkness yet not happy in the skin that is felt.

More praise given to stay in shadows and more threatened if left to fend for an individual plan, life not lived but seeing others who are bespoke from sacrifices made to be discounted in gratitude.

Breathing, Doing, or Falling Apart

Words being said to hurt and using vulgarity to cripple, hurting too much to talk in defense or gaze in directed path of such disorder; when thinking about what was never to be, or when not being able to think clearly, hardly functioning and numbness is combining to be overwhelming.

Not wanting to be close to love being scary and not being able to deal with a sullied state of insecurities. No caring direction and not wanting to start to regroup after hollowing out of a shell, to now be cracking and crumbling apart to destruction of what was trying.

Falling or slipping into fantasies and not liking reality just wanting lies to be told to steady.

Passing Scars of Distrust

Feeling pain when marks have shown what was found in discomfort of occasional exchange, seeing now what everyone saw to be as a reflection of painful logic that was far from perfect.

Closed eyes of trust to be now opened with disgust with fright to see what was left, pain inside that is killing and not leaving, trying to let go to live again come to find a fall again.

Patterns that show how needed change is provided but having to stop being misguided, a promise needed to shine and show pride to have faith in the sands of time.

Beastly Knock

Hearing what malice is thought being brought by convenient ways of personal trusted nature, coming in at ways that are welcomed through thresholds housing hurtful memories.

Invited evil and knowing what has caused the painful return of anxiety to a calming place, caged emotions that comments set arise to actions that bring humanity to levels fit a beast; all to have started from hearing a beastly knock.

My Own Forgery

You feel now that you could never forget, later it feels like it could have never had happened. Words are temporary unless you write them down, and memories no matter how sweet fade.

The road to your heart can be curves and roadblocks finding the right place to go can you ever go back?

Life hasn't changed, and when things get better others may seem to get worse, the balance of time and the scales of life stay in balance but finding a level head may be hard to find.

My temerity is weighing me down and finding truths in lies are difficult to handle when being attacked. Romance is dead, violence is it better, anger is justified but acting with hate is never just. A heart that gets beaten by love; does time ever heal or just conceal scars?

I am a forger of my life as I go, and my fate is sealed, just let me wait here and then gather the will to forget.

Acrid

Waking with such spite and not knowing where a life that was recognizable has gone, struggling to get a life worth the loss of distain that is so easily recalled.

Issues not seeming able to overcome to live in justified confusion, problems mired by actions unknown and sickness in a heart confined to be so bitter.

Hurtful Permanence

Quality of life that is crazed to find actions breaking apart by known explanations, cycle of functioning response to injured tactful departure with little responsibility.

Lingered accounts of nature that would seemingly add actions of deceit to memories, not knowing that pitiful behavior would lead back to the permanence of betrayal.

Screams at Anger

At what length of time it takes to scream out in anger can a soul be brought back from wretched decisions? It takes time to sort out the confusion that has been made from disorder that has been brought.

Wasted talent, with lack of usefulness, and lost youthful tract of time; yet still very gracious for what's granted. For a shortened pacing stride with weakness can overwhelm minds in conflict that can't withhold a disturbed soul; propriety has an end and steadfastness tolerates nature to subside in servitude with a willing scream.

Lost Light

Groupings that now all know the cost from averted conflict that where chose and lost, morals in life that have not been accepted what was taught, that hope is asked for a cause so noble.

Life's that have helped many but with troubles all their own, to be running from issues and cause harm, unknowingly at fault for sorrow, the guilt that is felt inside by many that have lost such a battle.

Mocking Terms of Society

Actions may be regretful in situations to make life more tolerable to suffer in an encapsulated way, awkward movements, and nervous laughter to relieve the tension of anxiety of intolerable places.

Terms of flattery led to sarcastic remarks to be suffered in silence and comments of ridicule so readily, that only led to a deceiving state of familiar instability that being mocked is an appropriate reaction.

Being so use to what should be inexcusable in a life that needs to be understood without luridness.

Missing the Point

Along the way of life longing for purposeful existence of a meaning and responsibility, with messing about of situations that has no direction and wanting contact but not belonging.

Nothing helping the extravagance of comfort from the calmness of a helpless point of view, somehow missing pointed paths to what was wanted from beginnings to grasp what was asked.

Forgotten Stars

Suggestions of what could have been and what should have happened to resonate with futility, being driven out by ill regarded behavior and a longing for something more substantial.

Hearing the diminishing cries from stars and held back of rejoicing lighted gifts, preventing forgotten stars intent, and holding back accountability for subsiding lights voice.

Entangled by Finality

Knot tied for a union being granted was their attest of such fusion with no evidence of betrayal given.

Presence of harmony and sense of finality, a path of what was saw with no evidence of brutality, not knowing that the details are to be more entangled by occurrence of relentless impropriety.

Gift of Going On

Feelings of life lingering instead of trying to let life form learning steps to let go of thoughts so troubling, living to love and learning to find a life worth the time to enjoy replacing the feelings of just lingering.

Needing the way to know that being fit to love is just letting go and letting life be more enthralling.

What is felt so wrong can be worth the trouble to find meaning to a life so brilliantly gifted to let life be.

Difficult Wall to Take Down

Inside the wall that has been built from bricks of disappointment to control what has been loss.

So difficult to let in the light that is needed to lead to paths that are saw from so far from grasp.

Lessons of mistrust that have taught loss in ways of foolish love to be shown so unforgiving.

Needing so little after love has taken so much from a heart that has built a wall so impervious.

Feeling a Demons Cut

Falling up through sky to hit a sheet of ice and not being able to breathe, air is like water when waking from a cold reality to a defeated spirit and incapable of moving.

Feeling the sharpness of a knife made from the backbone of your demons, a blade never ceasing coldness in spirit and too many evils to conquer; seeing darkness in eyes and deaf from absence of sound, needing to fall into security but with nothing to warm a cold soul.

Not knowing if getting worse or could be better than most complications of a disparaging situation.

Always

A word that starts such an amazing explosion of feelings to begin arguments with lengthy return, leading to such a disappointing end for both invested partners of a unified celebration. Sides picked for sake of trust with interruptions to hearts that soon lost track and then lost concern.

Hostile words to try to express needs and none that seemed to help with no regretting end, broken from inside and split in-between where two halves should have come together as whole. No matter how lives are turned, and faults being made into strengths, nothing will be the same.

Flooded Thoughts with no Return

Sickness filling and hopeless thoughts are enduring in a mind that is flooded with ill temperament; skies seemed darkened by dreams of disparagement that has lasted through times of endearment.

Filled a heart that aches from words of discouragement that has lasting returns of judgments, confined tears of unpleasant reasons of what could be imprisoning of ridiculed torment.

Unfulfilled

Going along with a life as planed with great design to know that deception is not far behind.

Loving investments to your plans so divine to have believed in plans of great design.

Seemingly to be accounted for position of unified pleasantness and greetings of endearing charm of a sweet bitterness.

Facade of calmness hiding anxiety of invented accounts of great length that brought you to shine.

Not knowing what can be found with hidden plans so divine with thoughts that you will be left behind.

Shining Sorrow

Having such sincere comments of considerate acknowledgement and knowing that deception is key, having a head held high and pleasant expressions of gratitude to be difficult to bestow and take.

Weighted soul and test of limits that has more pain than shown from a defeated spirit, shining through the toughest times to be had and feelings that have been hardest to express.

Hiding what is held in thought and holding back actions of a tortured state of mind in sorrow to only show a shining virtue.

Formed to Fit

Forced to be different than what is wanted and emplaced into a mold that is acceptable, living in a form that you know is a mold not made for you with any comfort as an individual.

Being easy to fill but hard to make your own with feelings of an impossibility to make a part of you.

Forced to make scarifies that will let you fit inside but having to let some of yourself go to make room. Formed to fit inside a life that may never fit, to find it hard to escape when trying to fit inside.

Losing Battle Ground

A life that has been unprepared for paths taken with misdirection of attentive study, finding guidance of misinterpreted feelings of permanence to have surrendered to deceptive exchange.

Kept hold of what was imagined to be true to find being led by the heart in a perilous battle.

Having disbelief that a heart was left open to lies that have taken more than what could be given, yet in regards of loss that feels like losing battles on ground that was never had.

Show Yourself

A wish you could not express and an idea that brings sham from a found part of identity, a shimmer of what is unexpressed diminished by past blissfulness that can no longer be shared.

Wanting to share a life with an impossibility that was once true to now be a foolish entrapment, blinded expectations of romance to be spoke in high regretful tendencies to show respect.

Contained Content

Desire that is hidden deep sealed tight wanting to escape with feelings that can't be expressed, with experiences of some improper actions with thoughts of those left out of comfort of contentment.

Dissatisfied with objectives to be a hindrance to quality that could be appealing if not contained.

Outcome of actions that brought such despair and now needing to find content in what is now given.

Motionless Condition

Undesirable in the form of inadequate life to have become faded into sheets of calmness, aspired to become more than what is given but life that has suited needs of such low standards.

Built up fantasies to have fallen short of sustained position in patterns of mistrusted aspect guidance. Hope having surrounded life for gifts of tailored limits to expect grace with age without provisions.

Unprepared self-image to face cruelty to harsher remarking of social torments to be kept emotionless.

Some Hear Nothing

As a wisp of a word goes by and answered a question that wasn't to be asked, a showing of what is close in thought from willingness to share what no one wanted to hear.

With issues that needed to be discussed with care and answers that are no surprise. Some hear not what was said but what was wanted to be asked and heard by all that are present. Answers given to questions not asked and not hearing what was being said with a closed mind.

Numbness to Regret

Defining moments that leave you so undefined in troubling systems of such defeat, from an unwanted character flaw that can't be seen only loss of caring felt by not participating.

Wanting more than what is left when dealing with life as standards are bound by reasonless charm. Reasons with doubts and feelings with nothing tangible to relay on when being hid away from growth, trying to stand on your own ground with needing life to be lived before life overcomes you with regret.

Dreams that are black and white that need color that fills an unfinished work seemingly dull in accord. Defining moments that are defined only after regretful situations have conquered a fortification.

Guiltily Attesting

Hearing and believing discussions of found love worth waiting but seeing life slipping, knowing that time is precious with days that have moved quicker than what has been prepared.

Passing nights with sleeping but never able to have restless thought of what could be a beginning.

Formerly being able to take blame to now displacing anger and boldly attesting accountability, being told you are wanted but feeling left out of what should be so easily had in relative exchange.

Seeing light and still in a dark place that's not worth pretending to have everything in place.

Guiltily attesting comfort in waiting and not partaken in rest that is needed for actions forthcoming.

Kissed Hands of Fate

A life that gratification is accepted of what was told with nothing offered to ease a mind of worry; aspects of stature that was thought to have brought grace to a soul belonging to indulgence.

Where lines have been drawn that if crossed brings the mighty to points of grief that is only encouraged disgrace, knowing what must be done and knowing what is to be said but only expressing perceived approval.

Stall

Finding that knowing where to go and to lead with care but finding it hard to share, time passing with issues that are a cautious affair and finding that pain is lingering in still air.

Anchored to memories by bonded promises that can't be helped to look back for considered reasoning, not turning back but needing motivation to move ahead to keep from stalling to release burdened air.

Possible Tolerance

Exhumed from an acceptable life to be put in a place of intolerable consequences of possibilities, burdened by developed situations of entangled tragedy that is seemingly a verifiable lifestyle.

Giving yourself to something that is so close that can only give rise to a tenacious love affair, only to be felt and seen in images of possible interlude to a condemning sourced trance of finality.

Cold and Heart Broken

Inside a cold heart shatter into icy shards that pierce a soul that has a hard life to sort through, feeling broken and pain of the cruel coldness to be found in behavior of odd and awkward movements.

Within where light use to shine brightly to be now dark and numb from coldness of what has overtaken, still and silent in frames of a calming life to be in appearance to be cold and be at ease.

Feelings of bitterness to be lost in a world to be accustomed to calculating motives influenced personality, becoming who was to be taken over but in a world built on timing, it may be just the right time to resist.

Stolen Comforts

Having to take what is out of reach to feel comfort in skin to control what is asked not to be controlled, knowing actions must be taken accountable for comforts that are felt so desired but not rewarded.

Settling in calmness to take what wasn't offered or holding what is not to be kept, comforts that are easier to take grasp with reasons that Justify feelings deserving of payback.

Threatened Heart

Having little to be threatened with if only asked to get what is wanted from a heart so willing to give, screaming out in weakening regret to have the silence screaming back in a full forced painful void, being so far but feeling a closeness in a heart of hopes that memories are to fade away with any remorse.

Needing to give what was taken when left with finality and stolen chance for sought comfort in known departure, locked thought of memories in a head with emotionless meanings are lost from where it is to be stationed.

Slurred Discouragement

Muttered ramblings to have brought words of such harsh nature to discourage influential unity, knowing actions that are took could be hurtful to find amusement from negative connotation.

With slight breathe sayings that need no clarification but needing to find understanding, not to be said but easily to come out in spoken teachings and not shown empathetic spirited joy. Ignorance is shown but can forgiveness be given to those who spread hate when not sympathetic.

Starless Black Skies
Some sought to change an image to lead you to restless blocked direction for groomed obsession, giving into their wontedness to let self- respectful nature decline into bred deception. Leading discussions to have pointless distractions to hinder critical processions for unfair advantages, going down paths that leave you in starless black skies with little options and paralyzing objectives. Empty remarks of what should be clarity to have given more resourcefulness to declination.

Evil Angled Attacks
Leveraged to move axis into evils with twisted truth of words of grace to obscured sight of purpose, attacked for advantage of corners and cradles of unkind actions for broken pieces of exposed weakness.

Trying to appease the huger of such evil attacks of horror only to feed the mouth of bitter courage. Beastly ravaged anger with hate infused disparagement of appetite that devours to gratify greed.

Trustless Distance
Extraordinary distance to do task of heartless betrayals is an embarrassment of such harassment, demeaning and extremely provoking yet nothing being justified to break servile connections.

Misled to a falsity that was to be a misuse of talent and disgusting betrayal to end trustfulness, disused service and losing a battle of engineered greatness for nothing bettering conditioning.

Devalued Life
Livid in actions that can be compulsive, saw through eyes that need to be positive without disruption, brought to be an unintuitive living after use is seemed to be an interruption from a way of progression.

Not being the best to be dismissed because of needing to be in connection with a world of delusions with disheartened paths of confusion to a system of resolutions of trustful impending occurrences. Felt having to belie on something that is not bettering the situation that seems to be devalued actions.

Infected with Anger

Having let anger control a life and infect others with such rage, toxic levels of hate build up inside, may mercy be found and not let it consume a soul so use to reticule and deal in giving the same.

Lost in disbelief and dysfunction have created delusions of justifications for actions, polluting the kind nature of people and what comes from such anger to be breeding of hate.

Cultivation of minds to be thoughtless and taking advantage of feelings of despair, a soul that was to be filled with light now to be corrupted by bitterness and lacking control, backs being turned can lead to evils that come out of the simplest of places with unknown consequent.

Sink or Swim

Needing to hasten pace to keep at a rate to stay from decline from a hard-working effort, sunken sorrowed vessels that need to catch a breath from treading in a narrowed given direction.

Living beneath values of expectations of what must be lived up to gain control of what is taking effect, finding living a loveless life that is easy to be pulled down into deeper water that is consuming patience.

Falling for love often but seemingly to look for truth in letting some sink into what a distant goal is.

Arms of Mistrust

Thoughts that feel safe but missing wholeness in dreams that are rendering to mistrust of certainty, to find thoughts to progress with stillness and wanting to fall apart in arms lost in time.

Dreaming cries of sadness belonging to disheartened nights that lead to reaching vacant stares, not knowing what must be done to stop having feelings of an isolated and hope escaping state.

Marred Comfortable Image

Darkened turned rout of comfort from a stance in silence to have thoughts of tainted temperance; darkened turned rout of comfort from a stance in silence to have thoughts of tainted temperament.

Falling back into what was an escape from lack of knowledge or ability to give up something so toxic; falling into an escape in a mind from lack of letting go of toxic memories that seem to consume.

Looking to see what is staring back at a soul lost in clouds of an existence damaged through time; looking inward to see what life has been leading up to from a past torn apart by lies yielding hate.

An image that uses to appear as if caring was present to not having clarity without bliss in a substance, imagined faultlessness mentality that caring was never present with cruelness so prevalent.

Shape of Hours in a Glass

Pouring into a glass to be poured out into a time of living that seems to cap off an opening for air, as the hours pass shape life to seem to comfort the needs to be accomplished to fill with exhilaration, yet to be left with nothing.

Details that have been ignored and no caring soul to connect to support a life conforming to fragile shapes, which has more in relation with revealing situations of mistrust than knowing hands of incapable feelings to connect.

Broken through time that cannot heal despair from lost time with little effort in a structured bond, shaping time to form to limits in your life to formed days of rigid posturing of successes.

Return of Many Faces

Abuse of powered circumstance and confliction of commands of incompetence, from who was to be trusted in position that has hidden deceit with betrayals of lengthy return.

Showing a face of loyalty to be in a portly raked standing with debating inlaid risks of exposure, inconsistent practices of teachings to what was to be so outspoken by such an animalized character.

Acquired Taste

Getting to know what a twisted sense of an acquired taste of living has always been. A life that is turned around and actions being deteriorating to caution with little forgiving, to show sides of what should be considered with an ease of comfort so unbecoming.

Carried with such carelessness and picked up with arms held such memories of fears, forgetting troubled thought to having times of joy in moments of sorrow from life that is bounding.

Laughs of love for what losses have been acquired when caution is kept at length of disregard.

Rain of Upheaval

A willing sense in such distress that makes overindulged essence of such disgrace, living that makes horrors of tragedy a force with destructive influence.

Stagnant ponds of gross negligence and divulged ignorance with distasteful acts of discrimination, needing to withdraw a thorn of hate to distract the pouring of vengeance out of such a willing creature.

Showering burst of clouded thought of what is claimed as truth is to only be ignorance, having found that only silence could take care of words, ideals, and actions of utter hate.

Solace in justice of disregarded rain of ennobled individuals over excised civilities.

Commenting on Possibilities

Foolish fervor of occurrence from comments made not for a literal translation into actions, seeing how feelings are harmed when in reference to what is timing perfect with circumstance.

Converting from immature nature to adult possibilities with trouble ignoring what could be pleasing. A dreaming vision that feels to have ways of guidance of trusting interactions with no exclusion, seemingly impossible and living on a trustworthy scale that has no weight in denial from potential.

Holding on close to needed release of indiscernible consequence with an advent of intruding unions, not saying just commenting on what would be possible if continued inaction from keeping perceived delusions.

Dream Mirage

Farsighted fragments of images that seem leading to conclusions of impending fate, blended dazing dreams of confusion in ambient sounds with ideals stacked unbending.

Muse less days and sleepless nights that should have been inspirational fantasies, getting what was seen in a mirage of horrors and foretelling of stories with dreadful endings.

Sold short of what is set in destructive nature and weary of life that has fleeting moments in time, delusion of healing that was thought to be leading hands but to only find prolonging a fading light.

Trapped in Shame

Many things that needed to be said to connect with loving souls alongside growing bonds of unity, bringing out fears that trap confusion in mindful belongings of personality.

Wanting a relatable life to prosperous certainty to give ease to pressure of delegated duties, the only thing holding back a borrowed burden is the shame of undeniable circumstances.

Closed off Ways

Not gaining acceptance in mocking gratitude and no way to manage levels of disappointed feelings, slight glimpse of encouragement to be closing out who should be able to see what is held closely dear.

Being more freeing to be closed off and inside your own head than expressing desires of affection, hostile disposition that is keeping some so closed out from a true acceptance to not overcome trivial faults.

Closing out and not including to be kept closed off in pensive uncertainty with no image confidence.

Consolation

Comfort that is not worth the cost of losing so much to be given little in return of hopefulness, praiseworthy prize given interrupted from disillusioned unremarkable thrills of influenced lifestyle.

With ill relevance and consolation of being the last to be awarded with spiteful graciousness, awarded notice but not given a notion of gratitude of importance with rightfully chosen remarks.

Double Sided Fated Paths

Hearts feeling guilty to condone condition of harsh accommodations and blinded by selfish fixtures. Blood vested of bleeding-heart society but not to a point of destruction of ability to helpful solutions.

Some with bitterness stirring and are finding it tiring to hold so tightly to memories with vacant feelings, double sided to keep proceeding and keep taking part of a helpful notion in prosperity for future.

A side destroyed by past that is now found many to be going through life unknown, to have fallen through network of cracks and forgotten for talents grown over by neglect.

Hopefully found worthiness in construction of foundation knowing how to begin with faced decisions.

Muttering Sounds of Disappointment

Muttered sounds of discouragement to have brought words of such harsh-natured disappointment, rambling about what actions are not took to ideals that are only in thought with no execution.

Knowing actions that could be hurtful to some but finding amusement from negative influence. Under breath saying words that need no clarification but need understanding if heard unknowing the circumstance.

Knowing not to say but finding only words of hate spoken when withholding confined bitterness. Ignorance is shown but can forgiveness be given to those who spread hate without knowing, being taught by what is seen and heard to not show a path of joyous spirited laughter encompassing.

Monster Pie Beat

Life being undone and lasting memories for an incredible laughable being, spiteful bitterness that makes life not worth the taste of defeat. Is it easier to be who you are to be with some terror and laughs along the way?

Being beat by rhythms of an unkind nature but built to withstand unkind works of a monster beat, seeing who is sought out in laughter of a beating heart that has more to give than give in to defeat.

Mashed by fears of uncommon glory and a repeated beat that makes laughter sweeter, having time to reticule with hate and having been beat by a broken heart.

Saving the best but having a tectonic heart that is more stone than glass but still gets chipped away. A heart that gets eaten away from broken beats of soothing repeated openness to heartache, bitterness that caused chipping away that has changed a beat of a heart so infamously.

Not Spoken Of

Strange dialogue that is not freely expressed with familiarity without opening of a life to be exonerated, removing something that spreads rapidly but not able to give feelings without returned sympathy.

Controlling with such frustrations with weight of passive denial of inability to deal with constructively, beneficial perceived measure if reasonable to ferry with strength in the ability to simply start speaking.

Not seeking approval and not saying any words that would be explosive but eating away of control of kindness viciously.

Covering Heart by Night

Emotions that keep screaming tears to force control on knees of objective consignment, crushing fears to a spirit trying to rejoice in living to shape a creature that is unrecognizable.

Being sold out for a lower asking priced betrayal of a controlling matter of worthlessness, not afforded a guide but let service be consumed by ill present intent without preservation.

Fears to be covered by nightly resistance of pressed observation and wanting a heart led back to light but still having a heart that is covered in hate.

Frozen Dusting

Frozen dusting of spiteful unbecoming behavior on uncommon grounds of disapproval, concealed notions of undiscovered talent being brought to highlight a surprising end to confusion.

Recovering from a thrust into unfamiliar behavior with needless disappointment in humanity, burst of lavender swept air and chilling unreasonable attitudes with awkwardly frigid stares.

Weighted Reveal

Getting lost in actions of plush formation of shaped denial in a present crudeness of ideals, accountable for actions that have taken place in regret and wasting away in self-pity.

Trying to take hold of actions to lead you back to a better self of not indulging in weighted activity, from beginnings needing to justify a life found in comfort in actions of unhealthy identity.

Conveyed Disapproval

Lost in victorious shouted wasteful commencement of partnership with greedy undertakings, of what was thought to be taken with relevance and to be found insecure feelings of inferiority.

Retention of hazy regarded showmanship of conveyed success in a gathering of kinsmen, with given words for grisly behavior without an out lashed rivaled clash of detachment, not being able to look in pensive eyes of found tragedy with only found remarks of styling of disapproval.

Pressed Darkness

Once a light that brought so much happiness and with eyes fixed on greed to overpower reality, finding life in a dark soul, and letting light escape that once was present that diminished so quickly.

Incomplete feelings and life stages that now has formed so disruptively that has warped sensitivity; ideals that were wished could be expressed but finding to be pressed in darkness shamefully present.

Birthed Vengeance

Coldness in hearts of madness with scornful knowledge with being told so bitterly of disapproval, suffering brutal categories of unequaled belief of returned furry from harmful presentation of spite.

Funneling pleasure of given identity to be gifted in posterity to being able to ruin truth severely, unforgiving junction of finding something inappropriately handled cruelly worthy of triumph.

Opening of uncertainty in a cunning service of beloved opportunity to victoriously ridicule, seeming to give into glinting strands of happiness with courage to deliver such spiteful energy, claim of flourishing hateful remarks of life choices made with a heart wanted desire for companionship to gain with means of vengeance.

Misstep

Fondly wanting such foolish luxury to be tempted by so many that has had more opportunity, to misstep boundaries and finding that circumstance has left you in conditions confining activities.

Knowing that hands could do much better than causes of damages to end with nothing but disaster, weariness in darkness that has taken over in misjudged lifestyle fueled with hate and horror.

Stopping acts of compassion and not realizing a life's call of mercy and deeds of great design to misstep into a nature of finding ways out with little decency.

Set in place

Set in place of another to be going about life in confusion and knowing that leaving is inevitable, shouldering blame of past to get to a point of persuasion to be left out of set distinction.

Having a definable life to live and sanity that is still intact but disappointment in life being brought out, an imagined future but knowing where settling has taken you and not finding a new setting so easy.

Having a true set path to find that is not going to be just settling and never to be set in place for show.

Step Back to See

Steps taken back in life to see what is of importance to issues that would follow, taking a step back to view your life in a different vantage point to see actions that could be destroying.

Tearing life away from reality to be brought into falsities that are too tempting to pass so willingly, to know change may be backtracking if not dealing with persisting issues before moving forward.

Looking back to see how life would have been to find that issues that would follow not matter what, living in what time is present to forgive what can't be changed and to know how to change wantonly.

Giving into get what is needed to change without passive regard to be so willing to give indiscriminately.

Storm of Silence

Calculated loves disaster from hurtful loss that is now a vacant existence in a storm of silence, losing battles with such frustration and concealed true reasons for leaving to pursue a fantasy.

Going about a romance with no regard for self-preservation and now to be transforming, then having lost what were your concern and your self- worth to be wrapped in brevity.

With paths that were left stranded and standing with promises that were given so heartfelt, to be found during a fury that is only brought silence to reason and feelings of betrayal.

An Imposing Disadvantage

A life of moderate proportions to be more forgiving to give into an out of the ordinary cause for a celebration, missing opportunities that are now of no importance and are only past occurrences to predict the future. An imposing disadvantage on what is currently held in high regard and becoming obsolescent, an imposed force to be dealt with to make what is to be presented a chance of change sensible to grasp.

On an own accord of envisioned enlightenment of what is to an advantage of circumstance, sought by what was in current standing to know where an imposing force is to be presently.

Feeling amiss in a world that is fueled with past culture to stepping down when needing closure, the ability to take what was offered in an offensive term of entitlement to great aspirations of reluctant change.

Stars Intent

Proud in stature but fleeing grace through steps that have wanted to help but have only harmed, from what was to be pride and in a state that applied unions to souls in protected culture.

Worrisome souls that need comfort in standing alongside obstacles in living from what is felt right. Stars manipulated to form to what is made from shapes that are so destructive in design.

Stars turned inside out and enveloped by a beast obscurely thrown in stars paths. Stars that intended to shine through the darkness that eventually consumed the stars brightness, afflicting the nature of helping hands that are to comfort that brought ease in time of need.

Actions of care taken of such great length to give reason for cause of affliction with attached similarities. To whom that it does not account for such brightness to intend to give the true intent of stars likeness.

Constellation of Suicide Stars

Getting caught up in a constellation of falling stars that needs more than willing to give in to guilt, hidden from sight that makes life so confined in a space so frightening.

Groupings of stars that are bound in a crowed space that is in need for room to grow. Fears that make screams of anger seem so small to the voices of ridicule that surrounds so loud; disappointed at life and agony that does not subside but voices that fade away so painfully, trying to hear the cries of stars and what they are trying to say but not able to give what is needed.

Feeling Cheated

Separated concerns of happiness and life of relief from confusion of a troubling misstep of sanctity, feelings change and can fondly put pieces of life together with new beginnings but still have standing doubts.

Deciding factors of separation on weighted concerns of souls searching for clarity in position, indignity bearing of concerning infidelity to truly cheat you out of happiness left with an inadequate life of unity.

Helpless in Crisis

Viewing what is seen to make since of what was done so unsettling in a state of incorporated fear, finding common ground that is feeling settled in an uneven balance of authority in tragedy.

Uncommonly stranded in strange surroundings regarding what was a setting of such helplessness to find that the end was more disruptive with disdain with little hope to be latched onto for justice.

Situations with no solutions that can ease cries or calls for a falling out of grace so abruptly.

Encouraged Words of Disappointment

Sorry to say that there are no other words to express the feelings of such complaint. Words of disgust, distraction, and frustration with single sayings of telling of disappointment, a saying of your own accord and dismay with the situations that you are fleeing to feed courage.

No found way to express feelings with validity and structure without cursed sayings that seem so vulgar. It's just a release of built-up anxiety and feeling of exiguity of life when in depths of seeming injustice.

Comparing life and living from distances that are so revealing in terms of endearment so compelling. No feelings of failure, it's just a release and nothing more than just a word or phrase with tone of expressed displeasure.

Blindness in Bravery

A blindness of actuality and deceiving body makes clouded judgment become real in bravery, not able to see the dangers that may be so close to exist in finality and loss so steady.

Blindness is only in relation to others that see what you overlook as just a fault of such bravery. A life looked at through someone else's eyes that can see a fall from what was claimed as an identity finding mistakes that can be forthright to a crumbling stature than what is an allowed inconsistency of greatness.

Shaping Life's Identity
A loving life of celebration and heartache to form bonds of sanctuary that seems no longer protective, disgraced and finding placing blame in a distorting attack and being witnessed to unsettling destruction.

Dealing with issues that have disoriented lives that have kept some from moving forward, getting closer to missing out on life from chosen distance pushing away reality with no idea of direction.

A world that is not helping shape a life with a desire to fulfill a more productive concern, past that comforts and familiar resource to help what is little connection with past identity.

Deceiving Darkness
Seemingly inability to let go of a darkness that is blossoming from past that still has presence, hoping the bloom of a dark covering of flowering shell will cease with deceivingly cold effort.

Darkness covering and only passive emotions being seen so thrillingly deriving from perspective desires, needing more than what can make use of beauty from what has been given to be so chilling.

Having to be so overbearing and can't be let go and move on with what is still left with life so deceiving to have darkness still in bloom.

Hollowing Numbness
Feeling inside that there is no more to give from too much being taken and loss of integrity, having the hollowness that only leaves doubt to be left with dreading being aware of affliction.

Burrowing into a soul of unworthiness to feel more lost than knowing how to overcome weakness, left mind wondering if suitable for finding a saving place of love to fill with an enchanting greatness.

Feeling that you have given too much to now only feeling numbness in spirit of echoing insanity not knowing steps to take to withstand such harsh beatings of feelings to endure disturbances of a hollowing certainty.

Bottled Worlds

Obstructed reasoning from words received seemingly to be real but only in surreal affection. Never closer from what is to be so distant but living in a fantasy of a closed off reality. Positioned worlds so closed and not up for a spectacle that would follow a misadventure.

Wanted more within reason but inhibited blurriness from demeaning vision within, nothing to be given worthy to be written to present so personal without getting exchanged feelings.

Breath of Hate

Feeling the breath of hate from words being spoke from beastly proportions that seem consuming, trying to stay out of reach from such created air to find that an obsession from a beast so easy to speak with such rage.

When what has been demanding only brings past hated breath to what was not possible, wanting past thoughts to bring smiles and laughter only to be overcame by delight in hate.

Trying not to get stuck in past thought but finding it easier to fall back into a place of comfort, winding back memories and making the most of twisted truth to custom cut reality, the easiness of disdain that is simple to explain without knowing actions were took that seem insane.

Mean On Me

Given confidence and wishing life the best of what can be given, not wanting to express true intentions, exploring harsh grasp with cruel identity to be showing growing potential but spoiled regression.

Not able to accept insincere remarks of cleverness and revolution of worldly discipline, remarks of felt breath seem too close for comfort and having to pull away from aggression.

Eliding Cries of Resistance

Cries for something more than hope in times of crazed fear and terrifying relief of sacrificed injustice, inspired by downfalls of charged anger filled designers of horrors with lingering clouded tortured souls.

Existent injustices to be established at times to now seem useless efforts to sustain resources.

Anger covering like skin that seems to infect specific innocence with relief of what was suppressing from edited content, giving back a world so wondrous to now be acts of attacks of freedoms that were the core beginnings from innocence to now knowing hate.

Screams from actions that are not intended to harm but invoke ardent life of brutality, to find that actions are distorting to lives that care, to go along with crowds that seem to inflict hate by the simple omission of knowing what would be worthwhile to face.

Prism of Vises

To be searching within and to know what is looked at in disgrace and what is shameful, a griping torture that is less freedom and stalling to unifying companionship within a situation of a confining grip.

Being encased inside a looking glass and seeing points of all sides of a growing problem is evident, exuded illumination to a point of presser to plan on separating deluding principals.

Seeing what is separating and unsettling to seductive plans with variegated light persisting to trying to delegate deceptions.

Backtracking

Going along without guidance may have determined disputes with directional forgiveness, stumbling back to a past that can end up falling into continuous troubling interruptions.

Going back to places that have more harmful intentions than progressive intelligence, having planted seedlings of distrust that had brought a nature so horrendous, a road that is easiest to be taken may need to be traveled along with a hindrance.

Fading to Bloom

Fading into darkness with a soul latched onto guilt that brings such frustrations, guilt brought by nothing of action just by circumstance with life succeeding in darkness.

In woods at night seeming to be by yourself nothing left but feelings of horror in your heart, with back turned and an obscure figure leaving sight until its silhouette is on black sky.

Flowers that once were brightly breathing in front of your path now to be desiccated, shapes made from the darkness and cold chills from stale air pass by with thoughts racing.

As shadows completely cover a body in night with calmness and at ease with what has bloomed.

Together Both Lose

Trying to stay together and too afraid to be apart, when separation is what has found to answer questions of harmony.

Too afraid to be without someone and not use to being alone, fearing what is risked from being apart and that loss can destroy rhythm so strongly.

Together losing what independence meant so faultlessly and together both losses so fatefully.

Of No Importance

Of no importance and not making a difference in finding what is needed to offer in a life of sacrifice. Taking hold of disappointment in what cannot be controlled in times of little forgiveness.

Much that still is needed to do and nothing getting to where it needs to be to find a loss of significance, feeling life is a disappointment to where it should be and yet not knowing where to go.

Wanting to do more and having more to do, just needing chances to be given when respect is received to prove that there is more to give than what is seen so lustfully from eyes of no importance.

Impossible Heartache

Coming to close to a heart that has not healed and what pain has turned into disdain, foolish to think that a willingness to change means complete, but to find time can be deceiving.

Not being ready to receive love when a heart is still incomplete and pieces are in defeat, shattered feelings that are hard to form to new beginnings and still too close to a broken edge.

Learning to start over from hurt and frailness takes more time than you think to an assured retreat, having a place of comfort that an ease of making life sweater than thought of heartache.

Overlooked Details

Apart from situations that constrain growth to whom you are to be or find paths of importance, knowing that tedious positioning of placement somewhere fits but not finding a suitable construct.

Not wanting to be more of an imposition from what was an imposing past of misunderstandings not able to explain details that would be questions that could not be answered from lack of knowledge.

Sadly, overlooking bigger impositions to let the smaller comforts bring happiness with attending details.

Indulged Group

Indulged to find slumping down and falling out of a shapely polished groomed individual, having ungracefully dropped out of the race to be the best that you knowingly could be, sloppily drug down to what is an uncomfortable grouping to be finding yourself aligned with faulty perceptions grasping hold of any weakness.

Now being in a common state of uncleanly disgust and being pale in comparison to what use to be seen. In disrespect with a lacking a sense to shine in possibilities and to grow with new opportunities, a grouping with lest likely association and accountable for current indulged activities.

Surrendering to Jealousy

Given into thoughts of found disruptive return to find thoughts of distraction and compulsion, finding corrupted influence imbedded in life's course with found fantasy of destruction.

Growing attitudes prevailing to made decisions with aspirations so unappealing, careful to not offend and finding to do injustice by living with surrendering to appalling rage with corruption.

Built out of Loneliness

Fated to be stranded but with loneliness that builds friendships from disaster in situational opportunity, amazement comes from solitude that was built out of an entangled path with unclear regards.

Having shaped imagery with wondrous story lines that was to be cleverly thrillingly enthralled, friendships progress brightly with a life consuming mind-numbing experience with brevity.

Having a distracting and tempting pursuit but knowing to be misled by faults would be disruptive.

Nothing holding back possessions of promises that would be inferior but having obligations made from hope from what was an overcoming of binding fears to be a divergence with seduction.

Condemning Life

With words that chastise without knowing and condemning to life that is to be caring still condemning those who just want to live; what is felt so lovingly to welcoming assembly.

Making life of unity unattainable to what would be an opportunity for loving light, various impressions given that take away meanings to what would be spirited rejoicing.

Trying to make a difference that seems useless in a fight for what rightfully belongs so humanly.

Loyalty criticized for what has been a counterattack of unions with such disgrace, to no one's choosing to live in fear and be held back by words that are unjust by any means.

Rising Evil

Invented contoured lives made with such distinction and attention to be taken advantage, aging bringing conflicts that have disparaging endings to bring conclusions that are uncivil.

Concluding that finding a separate way and not having dealt with impractical seduction, giving dimension what needs depth to find being pulled out by what would be paralyzing to reality.

A life that is not lived up to fullness divine in what is developed to be deceived by strangeness in time, something given that was prepared age inappropriate for lives of deception that has set in.

Honor that feels fleeing and taken by seductive hands to lives being interrupted but only in thought, weakness in heart and dampness in spirit with wavering minds that lets sorrow confine.

Unstable Beginnings

Releasing responsibility and a hope of what was passed down to not affect character, yielding to what control could not be enforced from what was to come from an unstable beginning.

From past hope and what is still owed to memories close to hearts intent to move from past offence, to make what was to be the result of courage to now be an irreversible dream.

Trying to belong to a loving heart's desire by memories that still leave marked torment, when desires are overcoming to please who is not important to future radiance and giving in willingly.

To finding wanting to give more than what can be taken advantage of such vulnerability, also wanting more than what can be given at times of distrust of stability to give into a structured facility.

Deceptive Agreement

When a head is being filled with cloudy judgment and no use coming from a wanted argument, sorting through a confusing realization, and letting an opponent form a statement, letting others be taking a point of view of satisfying arrangement that is thought to bring abatement.

Words being spoke that say they are there, but no closeness given with not knowing brazen confliction, saying what is on your mind to who is not hearing what is more of a confession, to find them telling you what they are overcoming in a lengthy statement. Situations seem similar but nothing alike, playing along as if caring what seems to agree.

Some wanting to say what they think you are going through but losing ground in unstable deception, there seems to be no base for standing alongside with a detriment instead of enforcement.

Legend Marked Greed

Marking what is looked at promising to endure what should be so undeniable to wealth, to be found troubling to be aware that some decisions are instruments of harm in denial.

No guilty conscious and nothing to be ashamed of with words of mistrust outspoken by actions, finding what has been progressing to be a release from remorse with no caution for protection.

A character that leads with discipline and has encouragement to leave waste to what was promising, marks of what were to be mastered brilliantly but being a vice of destructive nature being overtaking.

Loving Battles

Having to hold so tight to what has been diminishing though times of turbulence; holding on to what is so dear that brings life to the world known by cautious freedoms.

To the point of an end, so begins the rest of the beginnings to an end of a union, the troubling show stripped down bear with lashings of unwilling victims.

To now find everyone loses during the unwanted show to find spurious lives to live when fighting loving battles.

Falling Pieces

Pieces of a puzzle in hand with not knowing how to put into place and none that fit into place, a heart not having the courage to find the right piece from a fall that has taken wholeness.

A dream to be inflames from no way out of a puzzling depth and is getting farther entrenched, seeing a piece that looks like it fits to find more doubt in ability to come to terms with conflict.

The space that is left is more confused with not wanting to try and be filled with accomplishment, all around is saw how everything seems to go together with rules of their own accord.

Expression of feelings to relax in happiness of filth with a more puzzled fit into society, just not having the will to go through a path adapted for a cause for happiness with obstruction.

Difficulty comes easy with realization of loss of harmony but making it look easy to be so heartless.

Lustful Harm

Missed opportunities and wanting an appealing star to be grasping at imperfection, finding lustful light in thought and no action to bring caution to harming affliction.

Unhappy with visual seduction in depth of corruption of reasonable action in appearance of cohesion, needing to let go of fanciful and fateful thoughts of mirrored delusions to let go of lustful decisions.

To be lashing out in rebellion to find only damaging near perfection in falsified conclusions.

Not Hearing a Word Said

What was the start of a storm so wildly consuming to some that hear only partially what needs to be said, needing to be expressed in a preparatory manner to being lashed out at viciously?

Letting life be led and wondering why it has not happened more rapidly, not sure where it is going and where it will end to find that there is much more to be said.

Trying to show the adaptability in life and where life can be led but fought with no communication when not hearing what was said.

Bravery at Hand

Hard to wake and no need to sleep when bounding from bed in panic, grasping what was at hand to find disturbance rendering alarm just in mind.

Not able to get out of rational thought of being commissioned bravery to friendly advisory, to now being a waste of bold use of talented voice and with hands defending safety.

To be lost in a daze that would have marked an end to bravery at a hand of just a fantasy.

Behavior Unbecoming

From one place to another and nothing being denied on inquired position from allied strength, being in disbelief from what is asked and to do what was told thoughtlessly undignified.

Wanting to be given more with no disdain to find creating enabling crippling behavior, acts of selfishness and too confusing to be losing character when days pass with gratitude restricted.

Power influenced to give orders unbecoming of affection not defended but becoming alarming.

Lost in Seduction

Missing out on a soul-searching opportunity to find trueness in leaving familiar territory, seeing where problems are coming from and being unopposed to strikingly fight this losing battle.

Never repositioning unexpectedly to find a jumping point from a proclivity; diving into an unbelievable frame of mind that is only diminutive to personality that was so giving.

Missing out finding a lost life in obsession from where you left reality and a life of believing, so confined in seduction of a blissful unity that you are losing the first sought functionality.

To miss out on opportunity to be with someone annoying with tempting seduction, even if it is made from lies that have been so fun pretending that a life is worth the scripting.

Waiting for Resolve

Has it all led up to nothing, wanting to believe but finding it hard to believe in anything?

Sadness confined to a heart that is trying to endure, having issues so redefining to a nature so nurturing, troubled in transitioning and wanting to reach out but not having the courage to ask for resolve.

Being trapped by what seems to be unforgiving in times of reflection, not knowing how to find a pleasing rise to a life that has been waiting for resolution to be given.

Frozen Imagination

Disorder in delusions that makes a frame of mind easy to take but hard to deal with consciences, an imagination transpires fear of resonance in disordered intelligence and inspired actions of confinement.

Can moving on to greater obsessions be rewarding if feelings of regret from a life are still draining?

Transformed to seeing differences and still in great delusions that are freeing to actions unbecoming with known insignificance breaking a will of endurance if covered in deceiving coldness.

Inherited Faults

A cause for positioning in such a situation that will need more forgiving in progressing industry, drive in romantic themes that have led with melancholy beginnings with destructive endings.

Attracting an audience to branch out into the world with untamed vulgar proclivities, influential starts that become more part of culture than inspirited reverence in respectful authority.

Being taken in with open arms molding minds that need understanding preceding downfalls, cause of entertainment to be parts of ritual inheritance with provocative knowledge of faults.

(...)

Stars of Fait Accompli

Paths We All Share as One

The accomplished fact of certainty to let the feelings of needless anxiety to be taken out from control and letting an inspirited liveliness to give a turn from the worst despair in found crudeness of intentions.

Needing to live without the spiteful tendencies to try to gain the appeal of inspirited likeness of a dissevered enlightened appeal of gratitude and live for more than what is seemingly given.

From having a determined presence and more than knowing what to offer to not knowing what has happened to life.

The cause that is evident to an eternal soul and afraid to release from fear of the lashing of furry that is to be expelled with truth.

Travel to learn and learning to lead but still hesitant to release, fusion of trying to save with not wanting to give into a cause for fighting for a respectful victory seems needless when feeling like an undeserving character to finish with deserving finality.

Needless wondering about to not find a place to finish, the lost battle to begin with uncertainly and needing not to waver in decisions of bureaucracy yet feeling unchallenged can lead to a cause of needless surrender.

Purpose in Giving

Purposeful giving in times of more taken than what was to be expected from a life of spirituality, changing to give to a live that is extraordinary but only giving to rightful titled discovery.

Trueness in heart on actions that take purposeful living to levels of uncertainty in grasping reality, not just to anybody that has the ideal of deception in a life that is more giving than taking an identity to have a purposeful gift to give willingly.

Tempting Surrender

A meaningful progression without giving up what has taken longest to receive with honesty, not giving into obsession what has taken so long to grasp with no regard of consequence.

Imprisoned ferocity to be reluctant to serve silently to self-protected sanctity, not able to surrender if not willing to go beyond comfort of crudeness in accountability.

Envisioned languet lies speaking with such spite given rise to faulted temper with surrendered victims in belief.

Illuminated Cloud

Silvery cloud lining from clouded thought with judgment that hope seems to be prevailing, burst of joy holding trust with tears and fears of decaying marks of worthless connections.

Getting less judgment from unknown dedications to keep held in high regards of esteem, comforts from such harming lifestyles that need understanding with little disapproval to make choices.

A disturbing end to a loving betrayal to be given silver lined cloud to burst with love.

Fait without Doom

Placing your bets on a certainty that is coming into reality, having more comfort in heartfelt apologies, viewing differences that come to be critical to new beginnings.

An accomplished fact of destine paths to be where being lead is not of your choosing, fated accomplishment and what can be certainty with not dooming facts of predestine beginnings.

Closing In

So vividly closing in, the world that seems to be crashing in on what use to be so much comfort, looking to find paths that have tried to lead by such a narrowed way out of a darkened route for relief.

Filling in what seems to be the path of lest importance that has a world living alongside belief. Missing out to give others a way back into a life that selfishly does not belong to a world so greedy.

Fine with leaving the well alone and wanting to find a world of your own to fill and be whole again, not trying to shut out who are most important and willing to take in a different way to close out trouble.

Fallen or Called Back

An inevitable part of the beautiful life given, there is an end to the blessings of breath, for how we are taken can rule what kind of life was had by words of spoken identity.

Weather from the weight of a life of well lived happiness and a decline to a faded shell, to the deeds of others weighted hand of their destructive path and an intersecting fated fall.

Having a call to what speaks to the life lived can damage great deeds of mindful awareness, having ability to separate familiarities in what was known to exist with forces of discouraged disunity.

Fallen brothers and taken sisters will leave a void in lives no matter what will occur, timing being brought to end can also bring solidarity if the end was a timely demise with sanctity.

A Life Away

Feeling strength of a pulled direction in a goal that is farther than what is expected to travel, comfort drifts away when stability is threatened, and fearful destiny is headed your way.

Strangeness that is inside and knowing what could be if needed to backtrack from a pressing path yet avoiding lives that are parting ways from a route with little known where a heading is to show.

Hands overtaking a part of a nightmarish life that can only be taken away from assured security. Sickness that can fill a life if not known that hope can prevail in a direction that is thought to be best.

A life that feels closing in on passing years and issues that can't be brought to a point of understanding and a voice of reason is like magic yet still strange to find closure to who cannot see past a broken image.

Not easily recognizable to have composure in dissatisfaction and not knowing why willingness to flee. With questions inside looming that can be unlocked by healing seasons found in gracious living.

Action in waiting to find that time is healing, and it is never too late to start finding a life away.

Beside the Wall

Standing alongside of beliefs of true light of advised persistence with an amazing presence, guided with no words of explained actions that have brought professed expression of exhaustion.

Judgments of people that have no voice in life's confessions and offer opinion in lengthy frustration, never alone but loneliness that can be filling to an unexpressed heart that can't be explained.

Wanting to grab hold of what is still left but grasping a hold of what are lost in justifications still needing to find a path but not seemingly able to make way with the intangible truths. Seeming able to touch the things that were accomplishments and never to seem to get back lost moments that are lost in time or there are lines of fused potential to distinguish a void of romance. Seeing the boundary that is unable to be on the side of mostly sought influence but standing in denial.

Denying of what is seen so clear in a mind of progression and felt in a heart with desperation.

Guided Dived Path

Light with all that is seeking to be made since and sought to be released for all to see, a separation in what is taught and what is expected to be seen with feelings of where it is needed for you to be.

Going to where light may be found and to where the dived paths lead to find what is going to be freed, going down paths that seem off the laid road and following paths unforeseen.

Fulfilled Stars

Being lighted by the brightness that is cast by many of the skies lights with unbelief of beauty seen, with the sky filled with stars to show off the intended beauty of the most amazingly seen lights.

Brought within to overcome emotion of the wanted conquerable darkness that can be brightly perused, light that shines even after it subsides to fulfill a presence that can be a belief to shine within.

Peculiar Gatherings

Coming together in relief of living in pain to release grief that is being sought so desperately, aspiring for conjoined elation with enduring disparaging living to be brought to thankful retreat.

Plans coinciding aspirations in elation with enduring brightness in a prism of forgiveness, seeing crossing patterns of light in greatness and known destination of living in the presence of virtue.

Not a normal way of life to now people that play a part in a usual meeting with such grief.

Origins of Aspirations

Having light inside to have touched a soul to be pressing a dream of importance to direct accordingly, obligation of aptitude to bestow gradually to lead with grace and without disregarding origin.

Fulfillment of success to be presented from a light inside a dream of hope to be spread thrillingly; to find an indulged happiness with peace from willingness to be granted a greatness to give lovingly.

Floating Mirage of Light

Back-lit silhouette of flower graced birds of flight varied proportions of finely drawn lines of gray scale, looking as if flowers are to fly away from a watered pedestal into the night with ease.

Nothing being too far to be reached by an image of such delight of what is to be sought, starving for more than a look to have a moment of enchanted urging fright of unknown desires.

Airy strokes of pastel lightness of a mirage of beauty that gains distance with each breath, floating away within a mist of a nightly breeze.

Determined Path

A right path having promise with challenges in asking to believe with a nature untrustworthy, even if wrongs have been overdone and condemning natures are presumed failures.

In a finite world with little promises to be given to an unsteady behavior of infirmity, despondently inhuming in a final place of unrest with celebrating souls from a determined path.

Others that may not have a devoted path can devote life's to causes that brings light from bleakness.

No guaranty but a choice of what is moral is noble and to give up with little fight lacks known fortitude.

Startling Breakdown

Needing to stop filling a life with obstructed observations to get freshness in a tasteful life, jumping in unprepared with a heart that was to trust in faith and not questioning proceedings.

Mindful resort for a heartfelt openness for change of a life to have a lifted inner light, not having an organized life and not expecting to be thrust into unbelievable listed requirements.

With foremost need of conventional head turning posture in the narrowest kind of way, unsteady but precise timing to have a beautiful breakdown of soulful return into guided standings.

Not having the same chosen desires to fit in respectful attitudes that make a startling breakdown when seeing destructive influence from choices pursued.

Fair Made Glory

Not feeling faultiness that is made in fairness of glory and in a distinct state of gluten. Not broken-down and not yet burnt from a proven task of fault that was made from a victory.

Bettering identity to fair during darkened days of unreasonable guilt that is considered unhealthy. Glory not yet taken in and not willing to give up but is to have reason for fairness in task endured.

Not to fall, not to stray, to do and be the best in the worst of way to fair in glory from a made way.

Trusting Sound of Bells

Bells to rejoice and happiness to follow, you are asked to believe and to trust in what you see with life to come knowledge and hopeful wishes in images to catch sight of an underlying bravery.

Belief of what you know could make you happy and give much more than the sound accompanying, sound coming from fragile shape of flowers in bloom to grow into a feeling of rejoiced freedoms.

Hearing such bells fill the heart with warmth and the sounds of romance and long-lasting happiness, trust in the belief of feelings that are tempered to withstand the harshness of existence of misery.

Byline

Looking for fulfillment of love in life needing to write your own story even if it isn't a headline, a hand that is hard to hold and pressured to hold your head up through scornful preview.

Never a life to lead to unhappiness with a soul that is out of reach from skilled kindness, loss of love having left you empty from the ability to tell the story that was to end happily.

Not settling for anything else but the choice of acceptance by nature of independence.

Love Note Essence

Rose above the level of grand escape into unknown territory of truth responsible for guidance, with the ability to fill the full love note of life in what must be seen through eyes of greatness.

Nothing having more fragrance than the smell of a freeing spirit in light that has gave truth, seeing what must be free to endure the trials of life in the most uneasiness of circumstance.

Being so Brave

Fearing no matter what is given that no acceptance will be returned without offense, daydreaming hearts that are willing to let souls have a gift that is faithful with presence of bravery.

Having more to become than what is being found from being lost in a world with only disgust, standing out from a crowd that can be quiet consuming of trust when not willing to claim defeat.

Having been so brave to proclaim a victory in loss than admit defeat and withstood near destruction.

Kindred Journey

Inside light form differences in people that will not shine the brightest from unkind actions, when others diminish thoughts when thought to have found what is felt the right path to pursue.

Some having to go through more of life to revel a journey that is ahead to keep mindful strength, knowing what needs to be accomplished but having to stall for perfect kindred timing.

Waiting for a heart that is a star shined bright with the gentile presence of insight and delight.

Stars of Hope

Confined spirit in a hole that was left in a heart to be looking for a true fit and hanging on to regret, hope that what lies before you and a forecasting of a bright future with an end of misery in sight.

A twist of truth that needs to come undone to shoulder off burdens to get a well-lit heart of hope, to modify a fleeing condemned way of thinking to know what brings hope if seeking a way of release.

Come to find that all you needed was a hopeful moment to bring character back to an inspired light and a hope to have at the end of the night.

Holiday Light

Giving souls in such Great Spirit, past being celebrated, and family present, traditions being honored with love, and great light, celebrating with warmth and delight.

With the year coming to pass to start a new, hope of the future that will come to be that make happiness for all to see and to bring peace to conflict that seems to have no end.

When the New Year begins with bright eyes and new beginnings, giving thanks to a new breath and means to respectful years to come.

Toast of Unity

Hearing the voices that makes the world start to think and makes dreams possible brought together by chance and outspoken beautiful thoughts that seems to unify.

Hearing something so simple and unexpected that makes joy so close to your heart to have calmness and tranquil thoughts appear after confusion and despair form doubts.

Fleeing moments that brought feelings that seem to go on through expectations of fault and looking back through times that seem to make no sense to bring clarity to celebrated life of what was to come to be brought joy and delight, brought through times of fright.

The few that turned into so many that have cleared the way for the paths of light. United by simple toast of happiness and joyful thoughts to bring prospective of wonderment to all.

Empty Space

Waiting and doing nothing but seeming to have a void that follows no matter what delight has come, accomplishments that need space yet a void that sickens and low leveled energy that inhibits thought.

No matter what the confusion the effects of voided consistency still seem to confine what should be joy, closing eye in a state of mind that is close to happiness as close as could be found that fear cannot find.

Trying to feel something and sinking into darkness confined that space has yet to be healed from time, time will tell, and change can come it only takes time to tell secrets to heal scars that confine.

Having faith that your time is coming to fill the space that seems to be so hallow that happiness can find.

Possessing Loss

Precious possessions that seem as close to perfection as possible and to lose them unwillingly, when what was to be expected to last for your expectancy and beyond eternity to give in sadly.

Not expecting unfortunate circumstances that are caused to carelessly effect lives blindly, fated risk of trueness so faithfully belonging to virtuous essence that we all now possess the same hurtful lost identity.

Now to be inundated with cries and losing time to tragically fall behind a troubling possession of loss.

Stars of Faith

Stars of faith can lead by guided light and can help by lighted presence and delight in worthiness of sight, stops from being misled into darkness and can show the way back to the path to follow if led astray.

Starting to appear from just needing to have a glimpse of an amazing challenge to take hold so dear, looking inward to find what is needed can be revealed if wanting to know how to make thoughts clear.

Skipped Pages

Trying to know how life is to work before even getting a start to not dealing with issues consuming all thought, starting from the end to find conclusions on how to begin when skipping through troubles.

Wanting certainty with control on how a chapter should end to find a bother in whispered thoughts, critical of past that is presenting future trouble in finding destiny at hands of defeat of self-image in a mind that is seemingly lost.

Getting to a point that was to end to find it is only the beginning of finding out how to wait with dignity, finding some pages should not be skipped in life when mirrored opinions are found disruptive.

Feared judgments of who were marked unworthy to be more accepting in a path you are choosing just needing to see without a hurried   judgment.

Star of Fate

With fate in the stars and life in balance, once in plain view the stillness that was just silence. Outspoken words that were to show such kindness to be the only opinion encouraging talents.

Beliefs that will give warmth to frozen soul's consciousness a divergence from paths with hostile intents; future now to recover from desolateness and to deliver a life to independence and forgiveness.

To be given a star that has shown such brightness that with guidance led with substance.

Time in Service Given

Rusting without use and fading to be useless, running to finish with grace without rushed essence, usefulness to be given at will with brevity and years have gone by to stand test of time.

With ease and grace and badges of honor worn respectfully to be given honor of tenacity, so much seen, and talent given, but now to be withering away and faded into colorless decline.

A life lived comfortably and knowing that rest is waiting and a place so heavenly with light so forgiving, time sets in and never stands still through triumphs and tragedy, to be living on through posterity.

Embraced goals that give so much happiness and gifts of love returned to service given so remarkably.

Daven Daystar

Symbol of brilliance caught by skis intended light to bring favored gifts into sight, daily regard to what brings them closer to a lighted surrounding so proudly present.

In faithful return to offer and giving thanks in respectful custom a true sight in traditions honored, fighting ridicule and slander that the past has so cruelly scarred from hated acts of conflict.

Liturgies to give hope to people so true in mornings with brightness with a star that still shines through.

Reaching for Light

Times that have been seen in light but darkness yet to leave from a path not complete, safe trips are to be had and a road well-traveled to still be divergent paths from expected unity.

Many paths have ended before greatness has been discovered from lack of consistent knowledge; a dream from very little can lead many into a light of recognition of fighting passions.

The paths that had started can be finished with help of the dreams and desires of remnants of light, a desiring light that had been found along the way of a darkened path so not to diminish forgiveness.

Even if brilliance escapes individual talent that it uses to reach but now to be eluding touch of grace, open for the opportunity to join the search for an illuminated response to make a life complete.

Trusting Soul

Given and taken by hands of fate to believe and put hopes and dreams in with trusting receipt, worked for an amount of time in life to give trust to someone tenderheartedly to believe in immensely.

A satisfyingly closeness that is of such great interest that can be let hold of intense details in confidence, secret reliance with trusting hands to help hold an establishing of protected resistance from demands.

Coexistence with someone willing to help spread wisdom with diligence and lasting friendship, attaining positive outcome in purging truths into existence to bestow on a trusting soul worthy of respectful forgiveness.

Declaring Problems

Courageous souls with singular wish to expose an issue that is not easy to give or take with ease, not wanted to offend or not asking for more than what is expected but taking what is offered.

Hoping that living with attitudes that are adjusted to tolerance with wanting acceptance to merge, truthful words of release that seem to be music to minds that need to hear what can be forgiven.

Grateful to be given and taking much more with a soul at ease to fully discover underlying difficulty.

Comfort Pathway

Bound tightly by promises, was only for such a short amount of time to give up assurances, more living to do and more to get done to proceed in life that has goals far from present destinations.

Wanting to receive the glories that are promised and knowing that there is more to accomplish, anticipating beauty that brings joy and wanting to see a relation of past comforts to present status.

Having felt sorrowful but full of joy to have gotten past such a darkened pathway to escape ruin, hearing what is gloriously exhibited in such a wonderful pathway but not finding comfort in delusion.

Comfort aside and wanting to work through issues seeming severe to clear a path from past to present, such gloriousness handed by gracious acts given with ease, from well intentions from action received to form comfort in pathways.

Tempting Souls

An outspoken kindness to be an obstruction on a path that needs to be limited with brief contact, temptation sneaking out of places that can be unexpectedly finding a stronghold if left to same routes.

Committed deliberateness even though being encircled by temptation with seductive will, dealing with inadequate understanding of why change is expected with implication and no direction.

Release of issues that need to be a saving grace to be put in paths if falling for deceptive influences, unplanned betrayal is still in offence if left in the darkness but shouldn't be willing to take a risk.

In misunderstandings of change in substance, temptation isn't ignored freely when refused repeatedly.

Soulful Return

Brilliance eternal and lasting memories by earthy presence in a soulful body to know what is expected, rejoiced in song-like forgiving voices from misjudged past to now be asking for more than willing to give.

Inspirited presence bringing such a powerful way of expression from such a sorrowful occasion to a return for replenishment that has gained guidance form an amazing journey with contact surrendering.

Joyful reunions and blessings being bestowed known by smiling past heartache to choking silence, from freewill gracefully to be asking and betrayals are forsaken, love is given, and a breath taken.

Pastel Birds of Flight

Softening of hearts with lightness of pastels, which need care for what is being gone through in moments, aside of what must be dealt with that feels closer to a loving light to have an advantage in time.

Trueness will be given for such a softer feeling of concern to be gifted by flight of soul's journey, from presence of bestowed beauty and glory that has been received from heights not seen.

Birds of what look like flowers in bloom with pastel colors that bring airy lightness and life to stillness, calming and beauty of grace being birds of flight and colorful flowering bloom even through night.

Communicated Brightness

Unidentifiable obstacles to articulate to a part of a soul that is more golden than tainted by nature, grasping knowledge that has been faultfinding in task given with thought provoked questioning.

Acting on communicated brightness from unattainable security from questionable reasoning, seeking light that is found in souls of glorious stationing with persistence and forgiving nature.

With only actions to speak of and stories to give hints of fate in good fortune in circumstance, an obscured fractal of lighted knowledge that seems to have life with no sound to only be felt inside.

Incredible Grace

Finding to be in unbelievable standing in such glory to soul's fortress from harming influence, outstanding from unbending trust in self-interest that brings beauty from love of created loyalty.

Soulful debut of tolerant ways of relief of something that could not be given without a truthful heart, to bring bounding lives through dreams that have refracting light lifting an adored heart so gentility.

Hearts that need encouragement to move past the hurt of love that is past to perspective future, hopes of what should come to be so that love is waiting, and life is surprising when being trustworthy.

To be covered with sounds of glory surrounding beautiful accepting lighted interior, holding light in your heart, and letting love shine through the darkness that the world will show, prominent looks from the crowd with unimagined any other way of standing but their own.

Gifts that keep your heart from letting go of incredible grace that fills souls if destine for kindred love, letting the falls become triumphs and letting light be found from an incredible standing of your own.

Secret Understandings

Secretly knowing to move on with happiness and greatness that has been expected will be granted, under great thought and times that must be fought to keep from having a stationary heart.

Sought what needs to happen for life to move in the direction of motivated light with less to lose, peace being granted and togetherness with love to be helplessly holding on to avoid battles.

Having with great love and joy with helping hands but not to the destruction of life by harmful deeds, to have granted patience is not asked but has been proven to lack courage to move past understanding.

Secretly understanding that the battle is destructive influence toward unity and not wasting time, solidarity with shared light to be granted as a gift to not turn to bitterness automatically when tested.

Fated Rout

Being weary by the redundancy of overlapping feelings of judgment from a fall into deceit, influenced acts of uprising that make taking a chance on an abandoned route to lead to defeat.

Needing to relay on other skills to prove worth to not self-indulge from regret and needing relief, more treacherous behaviors to be dealt with what is being on hand from disregarded belief.

Urged the hand of fate by a glimpse into dreams and wishes to be learning tools and not failures, difficult to grasp if willing to let the route of failure be overtaking a true path beneath footing of faith.

For Love of All Light

Inward and outward we search our-selves for what we aspire to be and who we aspire to follow, no matter what we find to be true good, or bad we must justify our own actions.

We have goals to make our life better and dream of something bigger than what we hope to be, in such a caring way light is given and taken from who have inspired us or find who we have become.

Whether comfort is in our own self-gratification or spiritual guidance to keep harmony, loving our own light and seeing love of all light and inspire as we go from the different paths we follow.

Some unexpected falls through darkened paths we light along with grace when we discover the path, finding along the way that you need to relay on others to help you hold the light that greatness gives.

Loved Ones Embrace

Being embraced by something so big that consumes your life and willingly to be taken over proudly, wanting to be consumed by dreams that are only coming from past light that is now up to fate.

Knowing a course but finding to be scared to proceed with wild plans of accompaniment, thoughts with pure intentions of happiness and just needing an embrace to unite hearts willingness.

To be dreading what may bring disgrace by familiar presence of angered discharged from appearance, to finding a loved one's embrace to not only help hold but also hold up to stand out in confidence.

Eagle Wings

Persecution that still exist to some to be kept in lands of communist reason, with them not being able to return to their religious nation.

Lines of demarcation that have divided freedoms from what lands that have inherited people.

Cleansing of souls of ethnically blended culture that is still in season, fate of inspired souls to help the cruelly scared fulfill journeys to lands of a respectful nation, wings that help the displaced to find rightful homes as promised.

Distance is at hand and injustice fought by caring hearts, daily regards spoken in hearts to help return travelers to get to destinations wanted.

Before doors and gates are closed from unjust causes and secluded reasons, to help give flight to those who need to find safety on wings away from vile nations.

Caught by Mercy

Being kept by mercy with surroundings of past and no prospects for future when dwelling on loss, to be pressing with little give and wanting to have more with no shame of feeling unsure.

Use to thriving on happiness now gaining from seduction within a state of mind that is selfish, having to be bullish to have ways of constant arrangement to fight urges to reclaim autonomy.

Brought pain from what is persisting to a life of resisting indulgence and the found complacency, an attitude that is seeking to bring ease to now being brought to knees with dealing in consequence.

Fighting to come back to what is still in sight of claiming authority in respectful return to compassion.

Softer Flight

Drifting in flight above winter white soaring with wings stretched and looking to find a place to land.

Coldness frozen fear that leaves stiffness in a spirit and seeking a warm light to fight the fright, nothing being seen above and falling out of sight to stop what could be a harmful presence.

Issues in life that seem so easy to overcome and difficult to understand to find meaningless betrayals, hitting the bottom and feeling the stinging shock that covers crystalline hardness with bright softness.

Attractions by beast of such pray that are so unforgiving to devour easily and with no regret, being preyed upon to now being found sick with what is seen to be taken from caring hands of comfort.

Making hearts feel free and helps prove that what was spoken to be true to be found so clear, seeing how powerless to stop life from what is so easily to be solved but so many to now fall so easy.

Trying to make a comfort be felt to who needs softness in flight and not fall for cunning charm.

Blind Traveling

Needing a chance to show ideals that love would be enlightened to someone willing to share, not sure where the road is leading and needing to find a way to deal with sustaining reliability.

Going blind into paths that are dangerous but could be rewarding if willing to find love along the way, not knowing how to ask of such faith to someone unknown but traveling with plans to show.

Reliance without negative influence to feeling and taking time to care about daily accounts, something reasonable that could be enriching to lives that need healing from unknown fears.

Limited times to get what is felt to be right and not wanting to be made a fool of what is taken part, finding outlines to follow to make what is possible and making a way that is forgiving to faults.

Releasing caring ideals that are foretelling of futures unforgiving and dim to demeaning thoughts, blindly still traveling on paths that could be rewarding to receive caring actions that are warming.

Tempting Flower in Bloom

A deceiving body with such treachery sneaking out of places unexpected and so enticing, dealing with issues of inadequate love, or understanding to be finding comfort in a defending stance.

With commitment to have strengthened willpower even if you are being embraced to temptingly, so consuming that it may be fooling into an ease of mind of soothing deception.

Seeming to be a release of issues that you need a saving grace to keep from stumbling, tempting petals of flowers and drawn in by beauty that needs to be overlooked with a mindful heart.

Being led through fields that need to be held with hands to defend and to know what is at risk, for caring hearts to not be exposed to such torture and having to be kept from lush fields temptingly beautiful.

Calling to change lives if harming was to be exhibited in what was fought for and what is kept with care.

Finding ways of relief from what is pending to holding back outstanding temptation, seeing where life leads, where trouble will stray and keeping from grand fields in scale to what is gained.

Taken

May your prayers had been heard, and sins been forgiven. This
day shall be morn, for you have been taken.
Love for you will never be forgotten or mistaken.

Two Stars Returning Brightness

Two stars that are stronger together than apart even through brought conflict, that needs to help each other to await something amazing to be bestowed so lovingly.

A meeting of daring inevitability weather for an appointed union or known collision, following heart's desires to make fears vanish to shine with the need to help light the way for each other.

A match to be a pointed return to where an adventure was a start of lives so gracious, to return to where the continued paths of wholeness of loving light to share with greatness.

Covering so Cold

Receiving stressful content to have inspiring light to show pathways to be covering with deceit, life left stark for a breakdown to have a retreat to get needed relief and not a complete rout of defeat.

Coldness that has blanketed the path with darkness to show what evil is to bloom, letting darkness recede to a saving show of grace from insight of light to let love secede to knowledge.

Coldness so pure forming sheets of darkness to what a lifetime so unwilling to see was now to show, breaking cycles of feelings too insecure to keep from wanting to be seen that now is time to know.

Simple Comfort in Clarity

As hands on clocks turn and life is pressed into forms that have no molds with a set amount of time, no words of thought need to be spoke and gratitude is implied with simple passersby greetings.

Confusions inside and nothing that needs to be hidden just needing to be exploring questionable limits, not knowing where to go, not having any where to be in simplistically fashioned society.

Scented candles burning in what makes dimly lit rooms with only comforts of simplicity, memories being made and marked from lavender air so still that seems confining and comforting.

Calmer from what is just to be ignored and dealing with what is needed to bring clarity from obscurity, obscured fantasies needing to be shaken reality to core of belief of knowing imaged body of accepting to find a simple comfort in clarity.

Facing Fears

Moving gently forward to deal with parts of the past to take what is inspiring to keep progressing; trying to define what is now denying a life of relevance with an inspirited existence.

Searching for what has given hope and seeming so far from thought to have such pleasure, thanking the hands that have shown where hope was to be found that has been relentless voices that resonate in a mind full of terror from fears.

Having courage to move past what may be found as faults but are strengthening to character.

Still to Come

Having sacrificing choices in life to get to intended prosperity to now getting to where you are to be, to find your best isn't given until forgiveness of mistakes has taken place to control future dignity.

No respect for emptiness of retreat to where shells are to be filled wholeheartedly, honesty with self-preservation, and to work problems that have taken more to control esteemed goals.

Needing only to be selfish in care of what you need to be given to get return of prosperity, no use to any one if helpless in pity and despair to fall out of what love was given so beneficently.

Lifting spirits to be given more to get the best out of what has been made of life that has yet to come, falling back into former darkness and trying to give selflessly has tarnished through time selfishly.

Hazard Discovery

Finding that from your hopes and dreams that being stopped easily with deviation from hindered actions, nothing preparing for a life of suffering in silence and not knowing how to stop thoughts of shameful discovery.

To block pressure in living to not be used, to getting a good aspect of respect of discovery, and in finding that what was to be the most slowing of response to hazards are actions of denial.

Trying to find solutions of life with unresolved issues finding hazards from being disregarded, that is only negative thoughts that claim so much happiness to helplessness that are untrue to who you are.

A plea to have a recognizable shame evident but stopping proposing solutions of bravery, to only know that if given a chance light can shine through and let a discovery of life be true.

Wisp of a Memory

Kindred when needed use and denied esteem when nothing more can be taken, when so much has been used and nothing left to fight what troubles have been cumbersome to consume thoughtful resolution.

Nothing due but respect and honor to pass on to keep intended future happiness, spirits that have left presents of grace bestowed to now be a vaporous dream in a wisp of a memory consumed through time.

Piercing Light

Divided devotions and customs that seem similar with a purposeful fate in fleeting life piercing, dividing lives to have come to what are now to be directed but have common grounded belief dissimilar.

Fulfilling loving stories with grand devise with brightly colored stories that show rewards that are found, wisdom to seek what is of importance that cannot be defined by logic and touch but only belief of truth.

Sharpness of touch that has the power to change the appearance of crudely shaped individuals, to understand purpose in a pointed life of freedoms that makes enlightenment possible in piercing light responsible.

Punishing Judgment

Having a weakened façade to now seem foreign to a life that is close to ruin with opposition flourishing, the only gain would be the embarrassing fight from societal competition with unmatched damages.

An exhausting demand impacting groupings of conflicts to distance people with harsh judgments, judging eyes of ridicule that say more with peering eyes than what has been conveyed from expressions.

Unknown differences that have led to harming impacts of defeated character by charming presence, only to be found that gossip of disgust to be on minds that seemed so loving at times of a vile venture.

Salvaged

Traveling in waves of destiny has plunged what is now wreckage to be lost in a storm, fighting what choices have been made, and to find that missing those that had been perfection.

Forgetting the past that has harmed and poised to safely glide and wanting to see what was lost, collision with memories in loss of love in waves of disconnecting life of what now is offensive.

Salvage of the wreckage that would be troubling to find outstanding in crowds of confusion, never getting away from wanting to chase love to where it was left to find destruction that was found.

Not able to lively indulge in life or even live freely from guilt with traveled pursuit of past identity. To find that the salvage left behind is of no use to gain the reward of perfection.

Scalded Line of Demarcation

Great divisions drawn and has filled homes with horrors from cleansing of souls of disputed devotions, lowest standards of living that keep individuals from rising to levels with courageous beginnings.

Expressed loss scalded by hate in only terms of disgrace that grief has held with fated aversion, processions made with the need of invisible boundaries that bring such destruction by scalding a line with impacts of explosions.

Sun Set Serenity

Beloved view by matched destiny of daydreaming souls to encounters and searching in serenity, pulsed as one and finding shades of happiness to be found in smiles of firm belief.

Letting go of demeaning encounters for hope of reunion with a serine peace brought by virtue, racing hearts that seem to vibrate bodies entranced to an intense goal of relief.

A Voice

To rejoice, to give a thought an opinion, and speak out to what is relevant with views being disregarded, giving an essence to who are in need that has more to lose from others gain.

A voice to guide life because they are too troubled to think or seem lost in a mine field of confusion, from some who speak and say nothing, and some that shutter and have nothing to say.

When problems arise to find that what was said to be words with no clue of sanctity in a life of misery, unheard voices that are willing to give that just need a chance to speak if just left to think.

Crossing between Two Life's

Having reached out for someone that is too far from sight to be connected physically, crossing a path of great potential but letting it slip by and too afraid to depart from comfort.

Letting a chance fall through an opening in life to not be farther from where you know you could be; two that were willing to see where life would lead but paths laden with lies where tread, to look back with dread from mistakes that had taken away reliance in unwillingness to share truths.

Lives that are fused with seductive past that could be considered balanced if brought to see unjustness; a path that is crossing between two lives that is making contact difficult and separating feelings to connect.

Excluded Love

Knowing that parts of life have no use to become accustom when there are exclusions to happiness, a loving nature that is exposed so noticeably by all that had seen an absence in expectations.

Being excluded from lives that loss is felt, and being farther from goals than expected, holding on to memories is all that seems to be left and wanting to be included in surrounding life.

Being unprepared for much of what was to be accomplished and the need to expand horizons, bringing hope to issues that never ended, so an inspiring closeness can begin but missing importance. To be excluded loving ending with loss of importance with familiarity of knowing what is being sought after.

Unifying Relations

Knowing situations have solutions and problems have an end from what time has claimed irrelevant, wanting to have a rightful heritage to be given a forthcoming communication with unity so striven.

Now to be in a complicated position to having undignified approaching marauder in times of torture, a part of what life has given and happily conjoined with solidarity in relation to partnering with an equal.

Masterful Limits

Mastering the limits that were found at one time out of grasp blinded from terrifying situations, confined by overwhelming fears and not having access to what was needed in trying times.

Turning over a secure self-image to not let a downfall come to be repeated, overdrawn by triumph in a defending nature of worthily directions in a life so demanding.

Reaching heights that you thought you could not overcome to master easily if just facing true fears and limiting response of harsh actions when not knowing details.

Sparkling Beauty

Suitable bonds seemed to be formed but still to be shown inequality and a show of irreverent activity, luminous symbols accounted to such beauty having bright beginnings to be respectable company.

Masked from respectful company to boast humility in settings of seductive-natured opportunity, produced an individual further conceded covering to form a deceptive fondness to lavishness.

Filling an act of showiness and now to look inward to form shocked awkward transformative bravery, in need of changing sight of delusions of self-protected inability to protect sparks of beauty.

Timed Elusion

If never too late to start, is it wrong to wait and can it be too late to begin when timing isn't perfect; to give in when unprepared to end with amusement of regretted reminiscence of actions endured.

With a start to become a revised nuisance to a masterful art form of illusion in a delusional beginning; deceived more than what could be taken to extremes of counterfeit personality with vulnerability.

Onto new endings with steadfast beginnings that can keep from an outcome with harmful appeal, to end the falseness in calm bravery from what is disturbing in a life that is rushing to a downfall.

Simple Words with an Honored Award

Wanting to hear that you are more than what was asked and doing what is thoughtfully received, being told that you are worth more than what can be returned with no request to reciprocate.

Words being given with simple meanings that mean so much in time of needed celebration, feelings being vivid in a mind that honor is felt physically in seeking inward for guided conclusion.

With brilliance blistering defeat to come to conclude a shattering triumph with grace, being a point of light in a star worth the symbol of honored award; with simple words to express gratitude for more than what was ever thought your light could do.

An Empowered Pleasing Place

An adoring humbling light of a saving day of such beauty that should last longer, to be put in an advantaged rank with only thought of what would be best from sorting confusion.

Having the look of satisfaction upon your face when being put in such an empowering position, taking time to look up and to see that there are more needs to be taken care of than your own.

Receiving gratitude and learning to like the issues that need to be talked about while keeping composer, causes that need more than just words of consonance with those that have brought your standing.

Compassion in Place of Found Identity

Feeling something that is there and knowing a feeling of belonging but not belonging anywhere, compassionate response to esteem that recognizes glory but seeing illegitimate teaching of solidarity.

Not sure where to go from here and not sure what is happening when time passes with anxiety.

Asking questions that are up to an inner voice to answer with lighted response to lay claim, to have clear reckoning with traveled decency in a life of trying to find a satisfied leveled journey.

Where compassion lies and where identity is taken to find others looking for the same.

(...)

Ribbons of Truth

Something So Simple, and Yet So Hard to Take In

Simple guided knowing of identity can gain a more satisfied pleasure from living and learning to grow with intentions of clearly seeing other's identity and seeing loving guidance with knowing when being guided through selfish behaviors.

Something simple to say yet hard to navigate when wanting more than what is given.

Inhabiting loss with transitions indiscernible by prospects of future happiness and when looking for acceptance can cause a fall in bravery and losing a laugh of fun-loving brevity can mean a lost temper with bitter uncertainty.

With a lost laugh knowing that the inhabitant can have no title in certainty, life with a meaning must have a place to live that can bring happiness steadily with the findings of surrounded reality.

Needing Solidarity

Confused notations of disassembled truths that cannot account for lives of dishonored actions, being an easily distracted culture and not having the ability to see a path as a united group.

Trying to leave a mark of noteworthiness yet being selfishly gratified in undisciplined idleness. Not being able to face true heroism in duties to show future coming personalities a direction, needing the solidarity of true kinship to guide life when not knowing how to find the way.

Towering

So many ways to go with none that want to be taken in a towering situation of untruthful opposition, advantaged by privileged negotiations to be set in respected sculpted claims with negations of trust.

Heights that can be reached by so many if just tried and a succeeding light to be touching preservation.

Lies being laden coverage of superior knowledge and towering over institutions with selfish practices seem to have all what is needed to find that nothing can touch towering climbs of selfish gratification.

Taking Caution

Beholden vision of grateful truths of caring with extra effort with ineffective helping hands, withdrawing, and increasing caution for a wearing of patience in time of motivation for an advantage.

Not getting what is needed to move about freely in a system of ill advisement and fleeing safety, not needing improper handling and if not a solution, then just another problem being exposed.

Vision with Harsh Nature

A life of harsh discoveries in a fault-finding mission and being intent to find reasons of such hatred, giving more to be lost in what was questionable harshness to lines that were crossed.

Ideals that have taken much more and given painful discoveries to find love was lost in insignificance, not much to gain if willing to go without cause to extremes to give up life's comforts for brutal acts of indecencies.

Revealing Ribbons of Truth

A release of truths that has always been known just too afraid to show to anyone, feeling free in a form of brilliance that lets all who behold a new ribbon that has come undone.

Letting loose of anxiety and feelings that are entangled truths with false pretense, fears that are now just past anxiety to be let go of and now to be free to enjoy living; truth unraveling and very freeing of what you were afraid of two now come to be so relieving.

Leaping

Maybe it is too soon but thinking it is too soon to know if willingness means more than feelings shown; feelings that tear apart thought from a wanting heart and building a life to find which way to go.

Needing to know if time is right and willingness to take a leap for the path that is hoping to follow; inhale and let feelings go whether it is the best to stay as friends or leave to never be seen again.

Being Ready

Being ready for change and prepared to take advantage of a wonderful life that has been given, being ready to do what seems to be asked and the ones around are ready for change of perspective.

Being hopeful to give life a chance to change outlooks of lives with involved greatness, being grateful for what has been given and knowing the prospective willingness needed for results; now being the time to prepare to be changed and be ready for evolving into something great.

Ambitious Climb

Climbing an ambitious mountain of fear that holds something so dear to try and make issues aware; holding a light that has helped you to find tenacity to not give up when you thought a path was to end.

Tendency to stumble and fall on climbing on a ridge you thought was clear from trouble; darkness has grasp hold of a soul so tight that the climb is full of fright and lasting longer than thought.

Come to find a fall was not far behind, to stumble and be on the way down but did not hit bottom. Stopping from a complete fall with such felt disgrace that was needed to know what is passable; having found which path not to take knowing to find a path that is right to be bounded.

Yellow Carnation

A brightly lit yellow carnation lets remembrance come with such beauty, bringing life to memories and humbles the sadness that has been parts of so many; a memory that is fading and times never had that have torn reality, regretful of what could have been if such occurrences could have been avoided.

Flowers that are seen that were never to be handed to whom they are for, celebrating the times had and the stories heard of a person that was thought to be known; surrounding with comfort on days that absence is felt harder to pass with fresh perspective, not the only connection but making thoughts sweeter with crisp scents of life to remember.

Struck by Repeated Darkness

Repeating the same thing in your head reliving the moments of life that had been moments of dread, needing to scream at thoughts that bring such pain and sorrow to bend from a will of addiction.

Wanting to live a life that is seen and love more than what is being given or wanting to give in addition.

Missing out on more by inaction than acting on impulsive creation of daring dreams of production; nothing said that actions needed to be taken when darkness striking with no warning of affliction.

Actions of such weakness that are holding back notions of light that the depression of darkness fights, loosing grasp of what you know of love from crippling fears that has brought unrest to existing sight.

Fears Serve Disgust

Trying to show your heart a true path finding disgust holding back your actions of a loving light, having more to do but wanting to run because of fears that take hold of what have been challenging.

Falling into a world of service in disgust because of not having the will to lead on your own, needing to be forced to do what should come so easy but finding wanting to do nothing.

Not having the will power on your own to be a success and not being able to get what needs to be done, leading to darkness, and knowing light could shine but it's hard with only compulsive disgust on mind.

Steady Handed Judgment

In disconnected heritage of uninspired judgment on what is to end with grace, persistence to be imposed on by whom was supposed to be accountable for reasons of desire.

Withered opinions of overbearing behaviors to being charged with regretful accountability, studding actions from memories that have faint truths that conceal lies for protected confinement.

Needing attentiveness without persistent judgment for relief of troubling thoughts of unsteadiness, giving way to a harnessed power fortified by a steady stream of accounts of passing judgment.

Freshly Balanced

Never seeing what are in front of faces to do what is needed unless point of view is tested, misunderstandings to be set into jokes of appreciation can be taken out of context.

Changing a meaning showing what is to be said in truths of fascination without representing facts, level in thoughts and actions before attesting accusations and reprimand with intimidation; not bearing disappointment from treasured lives journey to listen without an explanation.

Finding a State of Comfort

Best gift to give another is to give your best no matter if thought not to be the appointed time, it may be best to be present in the state that you are in no matter what state of mind you are found in.

Letting feelings come and be who you have intended to be and forgiving what cannot be changed, the hardest part is to find where it is best to be to find the appointed time to grasp integrity.

Tiring Thoughts of Passing Opportunity

At a single moment that all eyes seem to be looking where you are looking, seeing what could never be achieved in form of lustful guaranty, not sure if what you are seeing is what is thought to be conveyed and being far from what should be.

Opportunities pass and wanting more to give into a touch of lustful acts of dishonesty.

Empty Prospective

Restless of viewing a past that had many ways to go but none taken to have uncertainty of future no plans, or prospects of the future to have no security in a life with nothing to rely on.

Severe dependence that should be self-sufficiency to have no rest in expression of anxiety, waste of breath in lifeless purpose with misery and tired of the supposed momentous actions of life.

Youth to have beauty to rely upon yet some are to be more lost in disappearing time with what was to have an adjustment allotment to being thrust into disappointment of reality.

Subject to Change

Drawn in a light that is detailing but can be lost in points of conveying facts verses ideas of oddities, effort on matters of importance to getting caught up in details that seem confining.

Having to dilute the pollution of all the detailing to disrupt the influences of opinion, finding if you change the chapter, it's more constructive to finding a related subject for reference.

Still thumbing for clues that are not prevailing in a state of exhaustion that is crippling, thinking of what it is going to take to convey your thoughts of resolutions.

Having only an idea of something that seems to be promising yet still very confusing, abstract contents that could be confused ideas of complacency with what is hard to find readily.

Come to find that it all starts with opening a chapter that you have been writing thought out of fantasy.

Confined Space

Intense situations of such stressful cohabitation with others that seem consuming restfulness, wanting to be relaxed and start the day with ease, coming to find that movements are questioned.

Actions that are taken to avoid interaction with some who are obstructive to views of gratification, finding to be more introverted in thought to depress anxiety of confrontation with meaninglessness.

Gradually going into small spaces to calm down frustration or leaving with correcting validation.

Life in Session

Finding issues of being misused and dealing with the abuse you give yourself to not forgive, irritations that grow to proportions not granted if not able to let go and dwell on past aggression.

Rotting sense of morals that can be hard to justify actions if retaining disgust of other intentions, emotions through acts of aggressions or retention of internal conflicts that end in frustration of lost battles.

Letting issues go and the belief in yourself to learn lessons and live with the strength of best intentions, finding where problems lay and then find behaviors that have lost ground in betrayal of inner sanctum with life in session.

Daydream Disaster

Lives so daunting and so unfamiliar that all is thought of are things that have no chance of happening, wanting so much to meet a dream and not just look in a window with undiscovered daring.

Still waiting for an impossibility that could bring happiness only found in a daydreaming daze, wanting to believe that what is wanted can be obtained but not in the life of living in fantasies.

So much that needs to happen and so little being tangible in true cruelness of reality, afraid in the most shameful way of unexplored desires all equaling to a daydream of disaster in shyness.

Plain Change

We go through life and along the way with wanted exactness to be revealed to develop a plan at will, plans to be not always what are expected but seemingly will become an urged pressured acquiesce.

A plan on how to be thought to go through life and altered route along the way and change unexpected, to see life turn the way that is wanted may never be or could ever be wanted so plainly with no cause.

Some change that disrupts and life still goes on with separation within a guided line of penetration, being part of other lives but changes may have to come to let life move in directed change of simplicity.

Looking forward to great new beginnings with knowing hesitance may need to bring paused influence, not knowing who is to say what can be going in too far or waiting from a safe distance of a final change.

To Get to the Beginning

After all that has been said and after all that has been done in life that seems to still be missing hope, it all may end to leave the ones that are unprepared in the darkness of pain that consumes brilliance.

To go into life to be so far from what was first saw in life's being started with hopeful perspective, decisions made that can find paths of trust to be given to unworthy allies that light never touched.

Life has built a foundation to encourage and not discourage with some may wanting to reroute abilities, still to be weary of the paths to be followed if being told to go down the same one laid for an unexpected fall into deception.

A life of passion and loving actions must start with trust and adoration, but having to be weary of counterfeit interposition's, to get to the point to where life begins starts with trust and doubt to confront untruthful telling of stories with over explained glories.

Cold Silence

Needing to be selfish and let feelings come to be shown to be able to move on with life, fears are compelling and feelings of being overwhelmed with anxiety.

Selfishness being the only thing that is being a pleasure with silence being the only solace from over exaggerated feelings, wanting happiness but only feeling the sadness drawing into a cold silence.

Learning to be calculated by dysfunction of being taught with displeasing features of hiding inner truths, withdrawn for reasons that it's just not the season for pleasure and knowing silence can be refreshing.

Closing off with cold practices to not leave a heart open for getting broken with penetrating lies; cold and heart does not open for being censured in ways of discouraged statements of niceties, trapped in a cold state of silence to live but not flourish in abilities.

Sensible Life

Thoughts going nowhere and not being able to let a thought of something new take place, thoughts of what has already happened and not sure how to make sense or how to respond to it.

Dealing with issues that are life altering and heart breaking to not get the point of it happening, only to try to make sense out of a senseless act of who cannot explain with lives unraveling.

Wanting to move past feeling of anxiety to a place to where life is relatable and peace is comfortable, a seemingly simple thing wanted and needed to get the start to a sensible life with applied knowledge.

Exhausting Effort

Giving more to find what is still to be learned is a great deal that must be accomplished, problems that need solving are going to take faith in essence that is exhausting battles of support.

Holding up resolutions that can only be taken to length of gifted gratitude with little reward, costly efforts of grace to find draining a last breath of concern to causes disconcerting of wellbeing.

Stolen Distance

So far away and not getting any closer to seeing the other to achieve comfort in status, it may be best to leave well enough alone and not tempt fate to cause a direct impact of heartache.

A feeling that is seductive and enchanting to be swept off into fantasy, knowing that what must be afraid of is the feeling of being inadequate for someone seeming to be so great.

In minds that would like to imagine the grandest of sites to be lost in finding perfection, feeling that there is not enough to give and not with conscious decision to divide the take.

Taking too much for what is needed to be closer to an embrace that has taken more by distance than stolen by fate.

Thinking of the Worst

If it could happen it would happen to someone that is susceptible to chaotic circumstances, the fear of this obscure thing that affects thought to be conveyed by nothing more than opportunity.

Accepting fault and being more accepting without justifying why thoughts are to be darkened, having accepting fault that cannot be changed and letting go what you have no grasp.

Taking the world as it comes moving with steps to come to leave more chance to have happier endings, when having the chance to take hold of something so devious to let go and go about your day.

Without thinking of what should have been said to give into the worst thoughts to convey.

Shaped Hours in a Glass

Details from defining moments that have detriment to caring souls to have damming impacts and shaping limits of time; not able to see what is happening when not looking for what is coming.

Broken through time that cannot heal the despair that keeps shaping lives with teasing remarks, as the hours pass shaping life to indifference from what is being willingly given to seek destiny.

A life that has more in relation of mistrust than revealing situations of gifted vitality to causes for reasonable assurance, trying to make time but not finding the ability to pour more into a glass and not wanting to enjoy life from the shaped form of responsibility.

Hidden Simplicity

Wanting to be something more in eyes that are a judging production of difficulties, maddening state of mind that cannot be understood and why there is no reason to depart.

Anticipation of dreams that are now on hold because of hidden fears that have saturated a soul, having no reason to be unhappy but not enjoying reasonable happiness to have a disappointing fear that is crippling.

Wanting more than what is being given and dealing with life as seeing fit from complacency, filthiness ready to be swept away or waiting to be hid by tearful days lost in insincere compliments.

The feeling of not being worth what is given being hard to take and even harder to explain, reason with no doubts and feelings with nothing tangible to relay on to be hiding from the attention.

Something so simple, and yet so hard to take in when nothing is gotten when given in abundance.

Destine to Change, Slipping Away

Thinking to be changing but just doing the same thing to have narrowing chances of greatness; changed path of curtain destiny to have found that the path was an encouraged destine failure.

Finding a restless climb of importance but still unknown and being lost in symbols of a corrupt status, losing yourself and still not enough to have a destine change in cycles of unequaled distinction.

Progression of changing life still daring to dream with destiny to change if unprepared for an abrupt fall, holding hands of time back from preserved greatness still not worth the loss to get the life wanted.

Not sure if it is wrong to try acquiring someone's approval if knowing that time waiting is slipping away.

Casting Off

In part seeing more than what was thought, having never seen faults if left with no willing to depart, there would be more missing if there were no issues with just leaving yet keeping level minded in casting.

Senseless actions that have a bad connotation that makes dealing with the surrounding situations trying, no use for ugly words to commence, but not sure what the expected outcome with all that is seen.

To now the casting of a mold to this unveiling to have partnered with daring and to stay enthralled, having no more parts of things that make not much since If the ability to deal with just leaving.

Having the courage to do, knowing that it must be done, and with sanity to be considered, for everything fits like puzzle pieces in the mix, and nothing taking place of who are now lost.

For everyone has now paid the cost of what is seemingly to be ignored when life speeds up, when decisions to stay, there is now more to lose when more people are now in the puzzle mix.

Putting off the issues of leaving, at first from thoughts that were deceiving to find truth in waiting, have now shown that there was reasoning and found a deceived form that was thought to believe.

If concerns are there they might be brought out, with frustrating anger and apparent with doubt, to be dealt with may be disabling and finding what is wanted and what can be left behind.

Cast out to have a form of familiarity either on specific wishes or with unwanted help, staying for issues that were at first deceiving to now be revealing the true reason believed from stalling.

With chances taken and a leap so unforgiving to be handled with caring arms to be hopeful and to grow, to a form that is now seen to be cast off a shell of disaffirmed and disabling to a true form of knowing.

Missing with No Guidance

Wanted dependence and wanting to have autonomy with unobstructed preservation yet missing out, not sure what to be without assurances of hoping considering directions with combined guidance.

With abandoning on feelings for what life is without the constructed assignment of accompaniment, with words being said but not the ones needed to be listened to by wishful thinking of consistency.

No assurances but what future offerings can be greatly appreciated for all that need to proceed; knowing with understanding is not always comforting and not possible when wishful thoughts plausible.

Still needing to be said and not wanting to be heard yet still needs to be told with not wanting to start, bearing burdens of life with no reliance on paths that are chosen without any guidance is never painless.

Missing out on much of what has been going on with betrayal on minds that can't be explained. Fear of what is being untold and judgment that will be likely to destroy alliances that are needed to give guidance.

Time Presented

To sit and wait and then go about the day, not much to say and not too much to do, waiting for something good or bad, this is not the life that was asked to have.

Having let destruction come too early from time that was presented to be accustomed, not wanting to be alone and not being able to be with anyone with any relaying importance.

Feeling abandoned and not wanting any help from gestures but finding taking offered kindness, help that is hard to ask for and not sure where there would be the ability to go if left with abruptness.

Detailing of living that would have to account for letting issues that had come arise from decisions, what was wanted is had only to not be taken but to be settled in mind felt loss of dignity.

Waiting with calmness and finding what was never taken to let feelings come with time presented.

Working Past Aggressions

Urging anger within those needs expressing, built up out of what is being saw as enabling, forgiven in a familiar place, and seeing use to be taken for granted when being prohibited.

Fueled with not knowing what has been compressed with aggressive tendency to lash out, trying to fight what is not seen and only feelings that seem to be regressing to someone unknown.

Not knowing where to turn to find what help is needed to pass through the time thought to be tough, working through feelings through acts that are giving and being something that you could be.

Found ways to get what is needed at moments but not thrive in what temperament seems to take, a lighted heart to rejoice in caring ways to give help to who you once where without the fight.

To help and be helped in ways of kindness and seeing what is needed to construct a kinder light.

Unhappy Mobility

Early on seeing that acceptability could not be promised but still trying to make it into formality, at first sight thinking it could be something to find that traveling to distances unsettling.

Commitments on adjoining destinations that have been promising to find nothing gratifying, ending up just hurting and being hurt is something that is immobilizing when passing a pointless return.

Unsettling deals of destiny that make a complicated play on tragedy with hopeless immobility, to now be unsettling and feeling so unforgiving to what bonds were breaking to strategies of reliance.

Choices having to be made that will bring sadness from mobility when nothing is accomplished.

Calling Out

Struggling to get a grip on what was taken out of context, finding what was thought to not be fact, betrayal of love and friendships that test temper to find lies to be on lips that were trusted.

Startled findings to be turned inward to start eating its way through details that twisted truths, toxic effects of emotions that at first could be great to now only are disruptive influences.

Souring of friendships and loss of love that had only asked for help to find all that's now left are lies, feelings not accepting of such disgust brought about by detoured directness of concern.

A star that could not find a way through the corruption of its life and peace in hope of light, one hand is wanted and the other offered but not accepted from fear that calls out lies.

An inner self calling out for needs of respect that can be given a second chance in a life of worthy compromise, life and love is not what was expected and not what at times is needed to deal with corruptions.

Names that are spoke of in detail to end in places of sadness that only needed to try.

Star Flake

Falling covering with enchanting glaze of distilling frozen flakes of crystalline haze, begin just to have ended the start of something so great to now in a state of disgust but found truths.

Finding pureness in levels of insecurity and to find to hold stunning visual feelings of ferocity, to live in harmony and causative to faults that bring misguidance but still to live so close to sanctity.

Lines that were drawn for love that have made distance with ones that were to trust wholeheartedly.

In life that needs acceptance without response of coldness with rational thought comforting boldness, tempting to make images that have more unknown than what was said to have brought such coldness.

Dreaming in a Daze

Being taken by a heart so giving, to find that distance was more than what could be striven for, a heart so sorrowful for love that could never been far from sight even through plight.

Hearts that have given but have been taken advantage by only the thought of what was to never be, mix matched hearts that love falls short and leaves imprints to linger in a daydreaming state.

Not deserving to have found something that was in dreams to be and places that still need repair, foolish to be open for heartache and pulled out of fantasy by reality of blessings not granted.

Not to be found wholehearted in hearts that are still to be so far parted from distance of goals, beating so rapid and being desperate for attention but only finding dazed in dreams that pull so hard.

With bonded love and befriended life that is now to be open for dissection for others to see set so far apart in lives lived in-between; hearts that paths just crossed in thoughts and aspiring acts.

Heart stitching embrace that has never felt a threaded connection between two hearts so tragically, hoping that friends will never cross with mistrust to find humor and not to scold that warm-heartedness from just a dazed dream.

Streams of Light

Letting light through to the center and trying to not get stuck in the prism that has found a hold, to jump with fright with bits of fear imparted by truths that streams of light seem to conceal.

Little purpose to a life in darkness and seemingly unraveling with disturbed thought with spitefulness, all straining emotions to fight different sides of what lives were trying to become without guidance.

Searched in the dark for the light knowing to have the ability to find but there are ways to hide, strength to go through with life and living with secretes in darkness and dwelling with private shame.

Knowing where to find worth in the path that is being shown to be guided with streams of purpose; purpose in a life that was thought could never have been seen to be living in territory of esteem.

Friendly Advice

Finding that what is given in true loving guidance and taken with care to not provide violence, having fun with familiar links in what is brought suggestions to needed relief from worries.

Answers that are more for fun than what life should be, but stories of adventures taken, requesting what is needed to find reasoning varies when wanted candid answers.

Points of view that are similar but not the same to have more willing harshness in common with the truly strange, being answers that may be hard to hear and knowing that it comes from friendly advice not to share.

Conflict that Confines

Conflicting nature that is not an embarrassment but others trying to have pressing confines, to cease what has made trouble and lead to conflicts that only bind freedoms when caught in lies.

Seeming to be wanted but no time to keep from rightful owner with same goals and expectance, racing to see who can get ahead to be the first to fall behind when lies shouldn't have persisted.

Having an idea that was to be found that life had other plans when choosing to twist truths around. Finding distance is best when attitudes refuse to change and needing to keep a step ahead of conflicts that try to confine reason from escaping.

Disadvantaged Pedestal

Dangerous in nature to find a burden in what has been so happily taken to mount in possibilities, decisions that are bigger than what was thought when acting from clever words of advantaged position.

A mound of possibilities to have found longing for breaking off such fragile heart's insanities, satisfying offering of what were immodest dreams of ravenous breath of fetching desires.

Desperately covering up a torment with joking irony to be thought of as equal partnered infinity; requesting what was asked for in torn promises with only to be left on a disadvantaged pedestal.

Untrusting Fault

Drifting back into a person that once was trapped in a condemning mistake from hands of mistrust, burdens beyond what is kept so far from keeping silent from trappings of past thought.

Fighting the urges that seem easy to become so quick in thought and actions of distrustful statement that is difficult to hear; past to affect present demons of inconceivable careless settings to harm firmness of future findings that it takes a victory in selflessness to give what could not be given from carelessness.

Turned Importance

The start of being a great leader is to know who to follow when asked to take risk that can be accepted; knowing what can be lost with aspirations of importance, but chances' losing what has been gained.

Loftiness is mournful when reaching farther than who is nearest cannot agree to terms you have chosen, turning faces of recognition to gain elegance in life of a trustful-nature yet potential to live unsatisfied.

Turning what was a joined happiness to be a loss of what is now a heartless disappointment.

Conflicting Stars

Crushing dreams that were to be presented to a life that was offering more than confinement, found to be rage filled and bursting from unknown places that are consuming kindness with conflict.

Mood altering from what is to be found to be shattering with what has been unforgiving torture; willingness to give what is needed to find that only conflict arises from disputes in paths so confusing.

Conflicted to bring stressful walls crushing down around stars ratifying with complaints of unjustness, wanting to find that issues to be solved but knowing attitudes will change when conflicts arise.

Leaving Secluded Safety

Stepping away from the remote loneliness to a life that has more importance with others, to not forget that life has a lot to offer besides the sought peace in a partitioned shell.

Having to test limits but not discouraging with frustration of closed off walls that has seductive safety, stepping back into a life of rewards and not letting past be a hindrance to future happiness.

Finding that what was made from necessity to now be a hindrance to progression with intentions, for what seems to converge what is held strongly and enduring strategy to make schedules work.

Seldom known to whom are to be such an annoyance that found irritable in times of dread, taken from a place of seclusion for what plans lay ahead and leave behind compartmental views for safety.

Coping with Bravery

Carrying of different weighted discoveries to gain notable charm through fantastic findings, being so brave that causes of harm are significant in a welcoming fashion when gaining popularity.

Caught up in theories of being founded by thievery to having to stand for falling icons of bravery, being in a sad form of comfort to be given chances of discovery and lost in victory with chosen elite.

Happiness everlasting to only be temporary in matters of treachery when stood by some so bravely, being stronger in words than in identity in powerless discovery of greatness found willingly.

Identity not holding up to a lost ability to form a standing shape of noteworthy valor so proudly. When coping with the bravery of doing what is necessary to get a clear vision of true power of self-identity.

Cultured Judgment

Disproved of the way that brings happiness by morality solely face valued by misled attesting, passing judgment without knowing lets known feelings of how provocation impairs justified thinking.

To find that more accusations arise from trying to solve personal liability with achieving hostilities, being something that could be forgiving that causes life to be interrupted by undo planning.

Taking part of a punishment that leads communities to thinking they are condemned from perfection, bringing normality to points of wavered judgment passing guilt sentenced by faulty mistaken identity.

To whomever is going to be representing causes obscured by tainted embracing inferiority; having minds with such anger infused guilt that leaves some lost and trying to find worth anywhere.

Having subversive thoughts without reconciliation between conjoined cultured judging societies, that can be an unfulfilled spirit and losing composer to be brought to verged compulsion.

Defining Symmetry

To know that a problem is consuming when traveled from being similar in nature to indifference in respectful unity, showing similar qualities in appearance with known differences form willing opponents.

Lining up visually to let more happiness show from life from lost opportunities to let go of regrets, through time the shared goals seem to part and feeling of comfort left to show only difficulties.

Needed to slip to fall back into arms of love that was abandon through subservient pressure, symmetry comparing the dividing light from happiness was torn from tragedy and madness of reality.

Movement enthralled by enlightenment to see needed fragility to show trouble forming, feelings that need to be thought out and a willing pair defined being together but stronger apart.

Marked Sweet Sounds

List that needs more than a mark by what is accomplished if wanting to peruse happiness, hash marking of importance needed to be completed to be used in goals uttered with sweetness.

Needing more time to find a way to make dreams a reality but with time shortened by waiting, knowing what must be done and finding progressing with intentions of forgiveness but still lacking.

Discovering that losing the will to move past discrepancies occupied by thoughts of absurdities, trouble from what is to be unforgiving thoughts that condemn and take what is unavailable to give.

Miserable shape and distractive form to not give the best to make happiness a priority in autonomy, no matter what list are promised and what must be marked still hearing dulcet wordy intentions.

Wanting to do your best when not knowing what the correct way to proceed with a purpose, leading to what must be done and letting things fall into place but still not seeing change.

Selfish at times to let things happen to be given what is owed and leading to downfalls unparalleled, trying to stop failure before it removes what life has given when not acting in lives in dire need of true fulfillment. Wanting what is offered by promises that were not solid proposals of future to end up marking wishes to a list that was to never be marked off by what was thought impossible to solve or too much to give. To having shielded dreams by words of kindness and not getting to the true propose of desires just a sweet pause of sound in idleness.

Flowering Acceptance

The brightness of such glory that brings sorrow to a place of knowledge and understanding, emptying out the stored pain from past blooms of such disgrace to find that beauty is in bloom.

Finding flavor and taste as eager from past delectable delight to now finding unlocking secretes, grabbing hold of what flowering beauty must give and never let go to breath in acceptance.

Sought prestige is what feelings can exceed when discouragement has lost grasp of torment. With flowering acceptance worthy the pressure of finding the needed relief of expression in knowing that guilt is never easy to free, yet less weight to carry.

Forced Exposure

A far and odd place of permanence being held in such distress of memories that are repeated thought, forced in what is wanted to be an amusement and relaxing time to forget roughness of past.

Knowing you can handle what life has granted only by building beyond a future of torment, to be giving up to a force that is seductive to pleasures with friendly advice with no regarding accounts.

Advice that needs to be taken with care and needing a heart that understands that comfort is gratifying, knowing limits to let reason take over when relaxed sensations are overwhelming with harming notions,

Going beyond times of relaxation to a time of needing to be brought to a place of forgiving.

Profound Continuity

Similar in devise that makes easiness to continue to provide promises to prudent revise; continuous in stature that makes concentrated clarity astute.

Profound minds convey restless thought to demand gatherings to depart with status. Finding sitting in place to be gazed entranced on studies abound; partitioned in life to gather clear reflection of what was so ordinary but gave such comfort.

Loving to Peace

Having to take part of a life and taken hold of all pieces that are part of a strained love, dealing with a troubled past and holding together what may fall apart at times through trials.

Opportunity that can be overwhelming when disadvantaged from inability to see loving truth, to find that faults that can be fatal to a life so young spirited and a heart so trusting.

Filling a love with pieces of past that may need to be released to find parts of life worth redeeming; needing to see what closing eyes of loving trust has given to a forced advantage to receive confidence.

Loving life in pieces without penalties to find a calmness of peace with clarity in a loving embrace for what has been made from past failures to bring success.

Opportune Disadvantage

Pulling back the second layer of skin to reveal what is near to a heart that can feel exposed, unprotected, and at times violated to be put about in a text of such humorous captivity.

The ability is had but finding nothing good can come from throwing filth to arm in conflict, speaking of in such a humiliating way to disrepute on vast platforms and potentially harm.

Contributed to a vast undignified approach to show disadvantage positioning of tributes, to find that you are a venerable being to have gone through with what most should ignore.

Disengaging Hearts

Finding barren waste to rooms that were full and echoing sounds of disgust replacing life, which keeps separate lives to no one's advantage and misplacing goals that were relevant.

A heart crushing fall to disengage spiritually from what was now a short-term lesson of trust, callings to have been paralyzing that stop discussions that would shift life's direction.

Passing through life disparaging and settled in through cracks of unfortunate betrayals, feeling alive and not wanting to end up alone but needing more than words of trustful recognition.

Falling in love for reasons that called for mistaken destiny to shift the wind of change gradually, to have hearts to flee from a union threatened by opportune timing to be tempered by the climb.

Rather not fall for something else that makes hopeless complications but choosing to leave regretfully, to now be a brisk walk back to an uncertain door that leads to promises that are not contracted.

Selfish Eye

Prize held in high regard and wanting to be closer to a rewarded life even if it means losing trust, trying to tip the favor of wealth that has been elusive with a delusional sense of self-worth.

When selfishly delegating and not leaving anything for others to have a fair share to find only feeding emptiness, selfish control sneaking out to take all that is seen when in an advantaged position of greed.

Finding only hurting chances of having more in an expanse of time with no victory from a costly gain; stolen in words or trust to regulate selfishly in great disgust to see what could be used for an advantage in the selfish eye of corruption.

Stripped Down

Striped down and covering up hurt to be striking marks of disparaged weakness to leave hapless in circumstance, overcome by all that pain and no restitution for what is left to consume when feeling misled.

Coming off as complete and put together, to find knowing not to take what has not been released, showing ways to give the best of what cannot be taken without a fight that shame wants to steel.

Being alone in a place so full, to be lost in crowded rooms that restrict air brings escape to mind, left curtain with eyes revealing that willingly deceived in a place familiar but awkwardly chilling.

Falling to knees crumbling to what is now a part of imbedded pain to choke on words that drain, broken by what life has given and what faults have been revealed to wonder if laughter is about you.

Knowing the best route of such willingness to deceive is only found with words of such terror, finding that in moments love fades away to turn into dreading to be close to who has betrayed.

Paving a way to new roads to travel with ease and giving the best to a life in need of loving support, finding ways to be shown praise without letting emotions take back roads traveled to popularity.

Worthy for honor and not last in line, staying hopeful and letting scars heal then fade to benign, hoping to find that waiting will give more than what has been taken, that seems to just take time.

Cumbersome Life

Flowing through bodies of great mistrust to fight to stay alongside with feeling great disgust; lying awake at night though hours of deep thought with unresolved mental anguish to never get rested compromise.

Having the need to dress down emotions for ridiculed actions of partnered betrayal, parts of life exposed to what would be now a modifying path of direction and forming resilience in uncertainty.

With penetrating wisdom and fighting through actions of abrupt confusion to find lives of separation, knowing what is to come and hearing the thoughts that are active around issues of cumbersome lies.

The worst has happened and now letting courses of loss be turned to hopeful resolutions of freedom in others unburdened life.

Angle of Grace

Standing upon the ground that is alongside gifts of shared favor; angles of light reaching the top of a great constant that gives off light from each division to show devotion.

Setting moods to give ease of mind that suits liveliness to parties of unrest, watching happily receiving inspiration from such togetherness to find losing significance in differences.

An angled grace of importance to give to who needs hope and compassion of different understandings to know that nothing can be worth the loss of what is held important to live of a familiar constant.

Venerable Elite

Changing practice without disruptive exchange through precedent of their own making, justified by status and blissful thought that make opinions seem rightful claim.

To being dealt with patterns of disloyalty by recognizable esteem to think more recklessly, labored life commenced into a state of ongoing battle for tranquility to have given into indecency.

Not being used to lessening into subdued channels by faults fused into dealings of shame, forming lies that make foolish detoured questioning to thinking won with impervious shadowing.

Fractured Image

Expecting what you can do by what person you see yourself as being and encountering possibilities, getting answers from what are only memories of what you use to see to what changed with lessons.

Getting past expectations of what could be to what can be given so proudly if expecting clarity, questioning the directions of what was projected from images found negative to find comfort in a real image of an imperfect crusade in fiction.

Trying to get approval from what someone else sees you as, and not what you are to be; images of the way you see yourself through a mirrored face of when you are in familiar company, even if it is broken.

Sweetened Deal

Answers that are going to be hard to take if wanting the truth but only willing to hear a honeyed version, grasping what is made from nothing to feel like everything is at stake in dealing with controversy.

Uneasiness in decisions that make offers so unappealing but knowing what is going to be given up, caution in time of need to bring solace so sweet to make deals with bitter taste that dwell from defeat, no matter what is given remembering that what is to lose if letting guilt rule the deal.

Thinking the best from ones closest but hesitant with doubt may be caused by unfavorable taste in a sweetened deal that may lead to disgrace.

Common Threaded Position

Being brought back through transferred points of separation to points of indignant behaviors, conducts that have more in common than what is brought to light as an inferred contempt for culture.

Common threaded positions in affiliated solutions in belief contrasted with desired forgiving natures, marred with stains that have covered nations that have nothing to gain ruled with harsh indignations.

Posture of being pleased, grateful, and ungrudging without judged frustration to granting release from tradition of a hazing form of belonging. To guided life ordination without insurgence of weapons to prove great powered elation in common threading for solutions.

Distained Failure

Nothing being spared from what is to come from disappointment that failure has brought, being marked with bitterness, and having a disappointment from loss that seemed inevitable.

Letting a failure fallout leave sight with no recourse to come back into the forgiving present, not a fall that cannot be handled with guidance but not finding what was easily seen if looked.

Having known where disappointed marks were found to not return a mark of disdain, leaving failure in past and future free to believe that there is a way out with little marking of pain.

Hurtful Living Investments

Investing so much into keeping pain close to a torn soul and having fidelity in full hearted delusions, with carried guilt and not seeking a conclusion from what has been an imprisoned loyally to pain.

Gain a release by not going in debt with what is painful in a fleeting mood of greatness to regret, having to learn to release what could keep from finding kindred living partnered presence.

Softness in Distained Comfort

Being closed out from friendly advisement and having been kept comfortable but feeling distant, not giving in to what would make you gain an ease from pain but have the pleasure of released concern.

Needing to not let urges dispose of will endure the knowledge of what is best ignored exposure, nothing being kept closed that could be an unforgivable cause of sorrow that lets a mind to wonder.

Letting go of distain from concealed comfort and not afraid to progress from a comfortable rest, thinking hearing what is needed to know that what is wanted is best for comfort from worries that bind.

Nature that will subside if let comfort impart to what is needed to be taught tranquility in confinement.

Encouragement of Rage

To have lost what was to be seen as a bigger accomplishment to lose from such anger in a fragile mind, with demonstrations to instill fear that could be frightening without creative deployment solutions for anger.

Having demonstrated the loss of composer that has brought ugliness with a discouraging rout, knowing outraged triggers to let feelings of insecure bravery not let an explosive temper start a fight.

Finding feelings of abandonment seem to endorse the rage that is felt so close to a damaged heart. Temperament that does not need to be kept in touch with so freely at hand to frighten with no end; meeting goals that may be lost if actions are not accounted for and needing to know the cost to not let rage engulf a loving soul.

Abandon from Preservation

Once close but now to be in an unfamiliar presence with unwillingness to share custody of feelings, abandoning preservation to give unwanted help but not taken as needed to find losing intimacy.

Finding the cost of foolish actions that are now to be the only means to safely keep principles that keep emotions hidden from a shared life to keep preservation; youth lost in secluded thought that could have been left with confusion that needed to find protection.

Trying not to be abandoning guidance from guarded seclusion but the only way to preserve thoughts that enlighten, feeling distance helps but missing security when concealing questions that is now consuming seasons of freedom.

Common Rule

More exhilarating to find a way to keep what rules were denying from consumption, not wanted to break rules but having more questions to keep trying to find an exception.

To now wanting to accept feelings to have no choice or if chosen to be left from inclusion, rules that are changed from being given with no questions asked from a disadvantaged concern to have bargained denial.

Finding in shared rules that are to provide safety from broken promises to need specific training, bending what is needed to take what is wanted is not an exception but an excuse for stilling normality.

Internal Misconception

Giving in to not be taken by a heart that has been misled to think that solely responsible for control, a misconception of what is close to a fight to internal strife that has taken lead to blamable downfalls.

Knowing to be powerful to have a misconception to not ruin a life to be grateful in tragedy, sought by difficulty in disbelief to find a concept that is worth the time to fulfill destiny.

To be shown a way out of conflict that leaves more behind than takes with no reliance on guilt, nothing more to lose but a belief that could be what saved a life from an inner sorrow.

Embarrassing Times

A chance of having a release of anxiety to be leading to jokes told wittily, missing out on much of what use to bring excitement from not knowing what is happening.

Confusion that was misguided effort to gain closeness finding embarrassingly answered detailing, knowing what was lost was the importance of freedom from stressed pursuit.

All to find what was missed dearly was closeness to concealed heartless faults in misleading actions.

Thrown Stars

Trying to find a route in life to call a homeward bound journey to a steadfast unity, stars thrown with displaced freedoms to end up not feeling like belonging to anything.

Pierced forged sharpness of unclaimed identity to fight unwelcome tendencies, inhospitable tragedy that has left scarred from defying artful gravity with deadly accuracy.

Benefit of Time

Not wanting to take benefit of misfortune to gain sympathy but having no options presenting, not a charity case or a bargaining chip without benefit of time to be a shelter to comforts.

Underwritten concealment of referred potential being rewarded to strongest life story, distance that can be unforgiving to be easily taken advantage of lessons of working around conformity.

Letting time take care of what can seemingly be over stimulated reinforced attitudes with ill judgment.

Protected Calmness

Wild yet calm in nature, beautiful in the only way known how, seemingly slow, and somewhat protected; knowing straightforwardness without annoyance might be a better solution than a loss in temperament.

Protected from the fears that are saw by so many and felt by us all just needing to let issues subside, breezy winds of collected thought to be given in case of exaggerated anxieties of life's affairs.

Protective features that can let air consumed in tension subside for efforts to sooth harsher reality.

Grouping Conflicts

Groups that seem proud of their understanding to miss true belief of constructed worthy opportunity, conflicted of response to answers that no one was willing to know how access was granted.

Suffering mind numbing dissatisfied ramblings of unappealing occurrences that have no bearing, a nature of faith to be looking for understanding and a nature of similarity looking for trusting unity.

Not accomplishing what was to be a combined effort to gain a truthful stance of posterity.

(...)

Coloring the Stars

**Falling Stars with Such Luminescence,
That Looks More like Color than Light**

Feelings that are needed to be let go, yet still must be filled with amazing brightness can deliver a sight of illumination to intended sculpting of light into shapes with confidence.

Colors that easily flow into loss can still be too bright to let go of knowing what emptiness can fill the likeness of what is hopeful to come.

Trying to see what cannot be felt may need time to appear in a loving embrace of confidence, just needing to show a truth of spirit to let go of regret and move past a point of surrender.

Wondering Mindful Color

Head in clouds tiring to keep feet on ground in a ponderous state of uncertainty in findings, hopes of something grand and dreams of something so wonderfully complete to be binding.

The wondering mind that makes life turn into something that is made more of dreams than reality, confused thoughts of something that is seemingly so out of reach and far from sighted potential.

When dreams in life are turning fantastic design into possibility with hopeful attitudes with destiny, futures that are brilliantly lit with prospects of what could be found if looking to find certainty.

Daring that could make black and white dreams that need color that fills perspective mercifully.

Lighted Dedication

Soft hearts feel and are receptive to what is needed for paths that urge to be taken with certainty with different colors of light to let paths open to guide the way that is to go free willingly.

Softness that can be too fragile to let go of what is not needed so it is taken, hardened hearts that are driven to task that are often confused with a conflicted nature.

Different colors of light inside make difference in dedication but still need to progress together, to lead and to be led by what sets heart inspired lights to a notion to gather befriended devotion.

Color Changing Personality

Going beyond a season of youthful indulgence to being inclined to matured happiness, to having poured out into a life of not caring and changed a way of life to less respectfulness.

Far sought change of a beloved person of respectful means to be giving more but expecting less, color changing with seasoned foolishness to be not what was expected with grand happiness.

A Shocking Shell

Cross hatch, crisscross, and cradles with precise movements of life to guided observance, painting yourself in the light you intend to be but being put where you are needed to recover.

Silent and vacant in thought, stillness in life, and no actions disturbing the fault line that runs deep, actions not taken and comments with no reply to be giving a cursing pause to needed reply.

Stilly eyes that care but have lost once rational thought and being stuck in a shell with disputes, past being present in a shell that resembles your own but finding to despise what is inside and calling your own.

Arms to hold and embrace you tight, not to harm, and not worth the harm to you to fight, an action that may come to the surprise by all and no more shocked is the one inside with the insight.

Content and Condition

Memories that have left softness and still make fond stories of hopefulness in progression, a life that is filled with actions that effect more that care from decisions in unknown practices.

Those who gave such warm feelings to help the necessary rise to posterity with forgiving loyalties, seeking help but not asking the appropriate question to receive care in finding careless satisfaction.

An undesirable condition that may be brought about by such weight of complementary union, being satisfying to lives now seems to have spaces to clear when aversion to plans that are dear.

Regretfully contained inside with clarity not found from reckless sounding advice preferred standing, getting deeper into a heartless act, and not disclosing a rut of unfortunate stems of betrayal.

Leading Strengths

Leaders that can follow and find where mistakes are made and own up to their actions; desire of emulation from their form of bearing to posture others to call to be just as daring, trustworthiness to believe in put all your hopes and beliefs in, to have no reason to not confide in.

Made to feel that caring hands are equipped to deal with situations that call for decisive charge, believe them to take worry away so safely living in a life worth breathing effort into a cause.

In ways seeing that life is being taken care that shoulder burdens to present an ease of comfort, with care and compassion being an authority to lend hands that need guidance.

In a great leader knowing who to follow without challenged behavior to forgive and not fore judge; led with strengths to not form opinions to make lives equal to encourage flamboyant unification, the fight for an appeased safety and to put resources where needed to fortify bravery.

Hopeful Hands

Shouldering off the weight of dread that seems to burden the pressed soul to hopeful discovery, filling an emptiness with illuminating hope that the agreement with natural wanting of advisement.

Accepting faults that may be more of an inconvenience at the time just not seeing significance, knowing help is possible to find worth in conflict that is needed to rationalize with rebellion.

Hearing the truth that rings through the darkness to be felt to ease the confusion of conflict, only the individual can say when time is right to receive a portioned control from limits of sorrow.

Delightfully Fit

Wanting so much to be with a star that is unattainable from grand space that cuts between, having once thought to be close but finding that pictures are delightfully sorrowful to comprehend.

Seeing what could have been to still be a fitting risk so beautifully presented in shaded desire, showing a side of such wonder, and extraordinarily sought magnificence of fitting spectacle.

Increased standards to perfection but still not sure if able to provide the needed symmetry in union, with such desire and in dire need of such perfect design that makes it a delightfully fitting step.

Comfortable style that is at hand and attitudes would be wonderful if to slip into familiar grip, needing to let go and change the pace of what was found in fate to give way to such grace.

Not a cause to have mercy and not a fit for something that needs more than what can be given, to be more like the perfection wanted and to give all to what will be asked if making a delightful leap.

No Guaranty

Unexpected and an unknown way of feeling, a meeting of critical timing with no approach, seeing little parts of someone that brings smiles and some shining glimpse of hope, no matter what is to be or what is in store for lives that have yet to acquaint.

Granted meetings with indefinite starts that may be a surprise with a challenging defense, being given so much and getting a chance to see what fate is keeping secret with design.

Gratitude for help being offered with noting that can be done for pain but to find a way to shine, shown a way out of a dismal path onto a start of a colorful new beginning with desires to lead.

Excepting to have hope but no guaranty of the future and dreams of what could be possible. Found and lost so much throughout life and now to find confidence in unexpected ways, needing to be ready for what life brings when not expecting to find balance with surprise.

Coloring the Stars

Taking notice of what is being said with no regard for feelings that are now found to be disruptive, stars that are inside that are issues of great proportions that need to be handled with care.

Concealed truths that love and a life that has granted realizations of eye-opening adventures, lies that have eaten away at a soul that was so true to form to now be disruptive in nature.

The disappointed shell that needs to have brightness in coloring the white lies being told, not being able to accept hands that need to hold with trust and acceptance and following guidance.

Kissing Butterflies

Having so much to give that needs to be taken to fantastic heights with the chance to catch butterflies, believing in what has come from feelings of body altering surprise to feelings that guide.

Readiness and willingness to be given chances so extreme to find that the other is just as expecting, nervousness in what is to be a meeting that has such anxious expressions of pressing importance.

Suited brightness in eyes so intent of directness that is empowering to life's desires to soar, physically exhausted and needing relief from feelings to be blinded by a surreal haze that is gratifying.

Truth being a priority of such a delighted presence when if ever rarely found importantly specified, with lightness in touch of coloring of fantasies to deliver a gentle kindness that is beautifully presented.

When emotions fluster and giving into strong delight knowing love at first sight from confident intuition, succeeding to receive a first chance to show expecting love can be delivered and given wholeheartedly; when first kissing with butterflies.

Doubtful Autonomy

Facing defining actions that have been a life of love to find having lost a part of identity, looking at what has taken dreams away and each day being consumed by other freedoms.

From traces of love to close resemblance to disgust, hardly finding ability to see the genuineness, having lost face in life and can't seem to take back what was identifying from what now is fleeting.

Levels of distrust in representing wishes of falling out from what is now to be a hindrance, finding it necessary to hide true feelings to fear hurtful interruption and may be disturbing.

Hopeful proceedings to realize that not accepting to get what is needed when being misled; ratified plots that have ripples from what is felt to now be only someone else's request.

Assault of freedoms to take deceits past what was ever intended to be to make a positive influence, now to existing trials that has yet to end but only start the same that has been presented.

An influence all your own and wanting to find resolve to the deceit that never was given an appeal, parts of life that have fallen to the wants that are not your own to find lost in distasteful undertakings.

Desolate Plans of Forgiveness

Not giving in to what is easy to find if looking for a harmful release but not wanting to forgive, a hurried approach to fear that isn't harmful just protection from reoccurrence from past actions.

Happenings of past to be brought to present quickly when nothing being solved from hate, having looked at what is in direct contact to find that you cannot see what is outstandingly backtracking.

Nothing noted that can give ease to issues that do not need to be revisited to find forgiveness, asking what is easily to be seen to have an impact that is worth overlooking in a forgiving nature.

Life with plans that was not expected to have to overcome in a caring supportive influence, knowing that you have not gone too far to find what direction is still in ability but no plans to travel.

Finding Greatness

Thankless acts that seem shameful to be denied settlement in thoughts so disruptive, greatness in not believing in words so hurtful and thought damaging to progression.

Being close to those who are deceiving and finding leaving the option that is hardest to accomplish, trying to go about the right moral paths that have led to such an imposition to lives debut of criticism. Finding no bravery at hand and bitterness is being distilled into hate that is so pure.

Finding that calling out mistakes that seem to have cheated lives to have rejected caring words, to seem to be only waste of time and energy to express feelings with no gratitude, wanting to believe in people only to be betrayed and treated with little respect.

Standards that seem to be so low and trying to forgive past actions from mistreatment, finding the niche in life that is best suited for the way of a minds relief from pain deeply concealed, trying to find reasons for a crude withstanding and not listening to reason but found bound to beliefs.

Others being closer causing such harm to those that still are in the struggle that was not theirs to fight, paths of greatness that are not found and ways of error so easily to bring to memories present.

Ambivalent toward knowledge and resonating harsh thoughts being prompt to account for deception, thoughts that have shaped thoughts that they're not worth the belief that they could be great, talked down to and now to be trying to figure out the depth of feeling that could have been avoided.

Through painful recovery to find greatness in belief of selflessness to withstand the bitter coldness, actions bringing clarity to thoughts and hands to have held souls pensive regret to withstand faults.

Tolerant life Possibilities

Life being a burden and not sure how to help if benefit could not be found to ease suffering so profound, feelings that overwhelm and have consumed hope to give way to routes of confused nature.

Giving yourself to something that is so close that can only be felt for a possible future, being close to what you feel with not finding a way to get out or putting yourself in hopelessness.

Needing helping hands that are saying they are so willing to give what is needed to feel worthy, not feeling that true acceptance is granted when not being able to grant peace from circumstance.

The helping hands are held by tolerance and are not accepting to lose a battle that is being fought. Finding being more tolerated to not offend and not letting the possibility of happiness from not asking the right questions.

How can acceptance be praiseworthy if love is to be found only in tolerance? Needing so much more to be given to accept help from something that cannot be seen; defined by groups that seem condemning that just want to help just need to accept grace in faults to let identities form with a nurturing hand.

Different Shades of Rejection

A simple meeting but not really knowing how to find a part of your life that wants more than what is being offered for returns in satisfied unity. Sadness when thinking of someone that is better than what you feel you could ever be.

Perspective in needs of matter of heart's desire and wanting to be equal in perception of love, shades of what make us all so different and what is unique but unifying to find specific traits.

Difficult to give trust and getting to know personal differences with no reason to resist, being so bonding that makes space between what is felt to be separating but seem to unite.

Such disappointment to find that the distance was never to be shaded in with spoken activities, to find that losing what was never had and feeling less likely to try again for fear of rejection.

Having different shades of rejected possibilities to not let a life of equal leveraged respects of gratitude have part of a simple dream to unite for fear of rejection.

Hopeful to Pass on an Illusion

Having fantastic fantasies in an illusion of kindness and then to fade   out of lives that have used up what was used to them.

Having life added up to wasted emotion without lasting love to end in delusional illusion of compassion.

Seeking the embrace that is so true and never to feel wrong to help when not as strong. Healing warmth that brings fantastic possibilities into lives that are in need, seeing progress in thought and in words chosen to now be put into action in passing delusion.

Stars of Light, Suicide Stars

Knowing that your life is more important than what is credited to you or your actions, stranded and lost in the world you live in, bigger hopes than what can fit in the space that needs to be filled.

A fragment of light and imparting of fear in starkness of emotions so incomplete, with a captured glimpse of what your life could be if you were to secede in life.

Strength going through with life and living with secretes in darkness and private shame, but purpose in life that you thought you would never have seen to find bravery in actions to dream.

Litho Stars

More can be seen through absence and less is lost when starting with just an etching, finding there is profound color in variants of black and colorless complexions of fear.

Prints of purpose to look bold in their shape with clearly sculpted lines of engraved markings of defeat, forced pressing of capture of torment of nerving chiseled truths of harsh colored reality.

Landmark variance of freedoms to repel past markings of shame to keep from a withdrawn skill, sheathing cut to form shapes of design to interweave defined desired form of circumstance.

Leaving imprints of past to mark on present to keep from having to progress through separation.

Tenfold

With hands of fate grabbing hold of something that could not be accomplished alone, forced to take time to find clarity of what has hindered actions of intended beauty.

Words that are received with more clarity of mind than thought was possible, so thankful for what has been forced to do what could not get done alone.

Being so stubborn to think that it could all be brought together without helpful hands to bother, to now be getting more done ten times faster and with readiness to be gathered quicker.

So obvious that everything was always there but was too blind to see it all come together, having to have eyes forced open to see and knowing where everything came from.

Not wanting to admit that grace had tried to tell but had to be shown with harshness of reality when a loving guidance is left to show through clouded thought and bring light through darkness.

Being surprised by what is hidden in forms of unimaginable creative destiny, thinking that seeing all that was needed and what had to be done to get what dreams were to show.

To find that what was given was in the dreams but in a way of others thoughtless creativity, seeing unfolding stories being an amazing sight but not seeing where it has been leading.

Letting go of fears and be the person to live in a new life unfolding to multiply freedoms to experience tenfold the charm of existence.

Coloring the Rhythm Planet

A retreat to the rhythm planet escaping from an encompassing rout, yet to claim defeat, synthesized beating hearts and all tension being released as if having been pulled in by gravity.

Unity from what is given to stars that shine brightly and forming familiar bonds of sympathy, sound forming from energy that fills hearts in electric love-based intimacy.

Finding influenced artistic lighted peak performances in highly sought-after accessory, of what is coming to be found of blended resonated vibrations to room's capacity.

Coloring the planet in shades of a distorted view, a repeat burst of fire assaulting a once humble view. Shocking to a punch of bass in paradise of rooms filled with beating heart breaks pounding viscously.

Freeing souls to be what is needed to let light become encompassed in rhythm. Needing to be helpful in a life of a frightened state of disaster to find relief, to sound forming shielded transformed bravery and found discovery. Ambient sounds of melodies that make falling into imposition to be fed with fears a past anxiety.

Needing the warmth of the lively embrace to feed an exploration of a defining moment, a colored impression of an emerging soul of luminance found buried in a disaster of self-impression.

A flowing rhythm, a retreating plant of sanctum to fill a void that was lost with loss of importance to color your rhythm plant.

Hope Withstanding

Dreams with vitreous resistance seen through with hope to give into meaningless acts of insecurity of self-worth to shatter. Color strands of faith envisioned divisional compromise to separate a freeing receiving of contact to have hope withstanding.

Straining to recover to not be taken down by a penetrated heart to have a hopeful withstanding, deceptive withholding in promises that were to withstand but now are ambitious failings.

Whispers of echoing truths in a hurtful nature commenting to bring about reasoning ability to abstain, keeping misfortune of destruction through invested suffering of memories and dolent recalling.

Holding on to strands of hopeless fantasies with twisted reality to not gain clarity of fixations, forgiven to move forward but often not able to recognize the existence of traumatic feedback.

Remembering what is wanted and forgiving brought harm to hope to withstand conversional pain striking throughout life the failures that are recalled that make for desperate reckoning.

Purposeful Look

Purposefully looking to find a respectful way of finding a way out of conflicts that confine, seeking purpose in watching details slip by and finding what life must reveal in passing time.

Reveling in opportunity that presents a sought-after appeal to make a life worth an effort to strive, not just getting by but making an honest try to bring happiness from light inside to spread with pride.

Standing alongside the purposeful look of inner worth to gladly see where problems reside, affixing an image of integrity to give into offered help and shading of a prospective light to perceive. All to have a purposeful look at a way to find that an inner voice of a broken conscience needs to have others' opinions to confide.

Lively Growth

Lively growth of greenery that covers for protection of the harshness of a turbulent wind of change, growth of an inner peace that shines brightly and freshly crisp expansion of generosity, no matter what directions of paths that need to be traveled protection can be gathered.

To give thoughtful exchange for a return of favored existence to turn blindness to deficiencies, not seeing what is wrong with paring of unity to need to have an opening of eyes of resistance.

Protection from excessive uncontrollable cruelness with greedily undertones of misuse of kindness, to give what is needed to get explanations of what use to be vulgarities in eyes of opponents.

Giving into greatness not yet defined by the structure of a sharpened wit of intrigue, still needing help to guide away from positions that are continually threatening a nature of stupidity, to ghastly gains of overindulged soliciting of an opportunity that has presented but letting slide proudly.

Aware of unsatisfied behavior to recall comments of a lustful light to blind side respect, trying to take what has taken a lifetime to protect and needing to be ignored with delight.

Having lost identity to a regretful point of view to now being more forgiving than given credit, a brotherly loving enduring climb to heartfelt apologies to make up for loss of etiquette, to hopefully be forgiven for not being aware of what has been taken and now knowing true respect.

The Capture of Consuming Pleasure

The stars so rapidly consuming concept of a knowing way of failure to prolonged torture, pass the prime of indifference to guide with luster to only shine brighter than thought possible.

Consuming brilliance to last for an increasing amount of time to linger in concealing time, blue cascading trails of deception that makes it hard to know direction of a pursuit of an intended fall.

Before loss of light is to burn out from loss of intent to keep shining so bright, the capture of consuming nature in a pleasured fight to bring down with harshness of flight in disaster.

Having an exception to a rule that pleasure is to matter to increase fulfillment of desire.

A Look of Concern

Not knowing why being confused by complexity and disappointed by faulty misconceptions, knowing that issues have taken away from direction and not wanting to look back with disdain.

A pierced look of pale blue into eyes of an unknowing substitute of what was really wanted, not sure why or how things worked out and how it affects now that there are looks of concern.

Nothing as to harsh to have quantified this retreat to preserve a loss of backing projected faults, when speaking up causes more harm than good and looking back only leaves distain in acts to follow.

Faith being part of knowing and others to think they have the answer that is to govern worldly concerns, to merger with quality to gain wanted posterity with the concerning look of fidelity in lies.

Comfort in a Colorless Complexion

Heartfelt apologies mean nothing when left to fend off darkness in unprepared solitude, not knowing how to get done what is wanted and not sure if burdens can be taken if not shared.

Colorless complexion fading away into unfamiliar territory in realization of grasping loneliness, asking questions, and defining a solution that is made by unique qualities of frustration.

Put together in ways of honesty the only way that can be for a sought- after integrity, having to find what makes life better but not sure if after an approval or is it just a need of surrender.

An indignant behavior that can hurt from scaring breath of arguments that is an obstruction, finding a better color to fit into is difficult when searching in the same area of disapproval.

Fading into a color of non-importance and not relevant in a blinding cause of torment, come to find some of the most revered times to come from the most heart shattering moments.

Letting heads rest in comfort on false realizations to relax in a fascination of found self-identification, comfort in colorless complexion when left out in a cold direction of immobilization of actions.

Traveling ahead to make your own way with strength from an unknown place with bounding principles; comfort in color even if it seems to be pale and has lost volume of worth in complexion.

Repeated Patterns

Patterns that lead life in a way of unremarkable behavior and led to an unforgiving nature, seeing what is being a repeated story to have a pattern of no possible variety.

Walked away to find something better but come back to try to fit into a life that is not suitable, only to fall back into patterns that has led away from turning to a true validated principal.

Wavering back to where comfort lies to become accustomed to settling into an unsatisfied character, not fitting were trying to reside and uneasiness in an unaccepted presence of disturbing laughter.

Kept looking for what is needed and wanting to be accepted for the way of an accustomed liberation, only needed, and looking for something that can't be accepted to be taken advantage of a naïve hope.

Having strength confined for an advantaged find for a takeover in a simplistic mind of a wanting dream, accepting nothing less than true acceptance or giving up when losing a fighting chance to gain dominance.

Needing to See

Needing to feel, needing to see what is evident by all except for who oversees deciding factors, not seeing what is needed to become what was to be and to feel what is right to go on through.

The leftover parts of life in past memory to be lost in actions of not understanding what was to be done, nothing being a willing decline and not knowing how to gain the affection of familiar acceptance.

Parts of a life that was to show love with little guidance when not knowing what is happening, most of insecurity to be frightening to come to see that what was needed to be done is not easy to do.

Needing to see, needing to feel that what is to come can be gained through accepting consequence, actions that are coming with love and respect to granted protection from fearing harmful actions.

Happened by chance to give sight that could not be seen on levels of insecurity to gain certainty, not knowing what is being seen by shaded infidelity to be lost in hopeful integrity.

Instead of being shown direction to be hidden by lies that everything has been finely tuned bravery just needing to see with willing eyes.

Centered Bravery

Coming from a centered body of efferent energy to strengthen support of collective knowledge, precise timing of a needed show of qualities in bravery and strength from a center to have prosperity. Hopeful return of loving essence that brings closeness to a place of felt inner guidance.

A basic sharing of forgiveness with a proclaimed jubilance in respect of a return to greatness, having the opportune timing of integrity to get the needed support of generosity with a guided calling, an approaching middle of serenity to be spoken in different forms of communicated brightness.

Learning when in need to substitute for a necessity to give inner strength with clarity to gain ground, afferent darkness hindering progression with insecurities to intrude with dishonored reputation.

Seeking sanctuary to provide the needed recovery from indecency to gain stability to reverent society; coming to an understanding to fulfill substantial discussions of importance with hopeful gratitude.

Effervescently gaining self-approval and to have regard to center bravery to deal with strained relations with no backing of certitude.

Justice Beyond Sacrifice

Given up fantasy to truth in identity with the need to show a turned redeeming face of responsibility, removing excuses from an injustice to have rightful claim of identity in autonomy.

Nothing beyond sacrifice to get a definite greatness in eyes that seem to gaze up in respectful honor, freedoms to be found locked in thought and no actions being able to release from bonded restraints.

Processed through systems of cruel deciding factors of willingness to sacrifice justice, sometimes people need an excuse for getting help to gain a reasonable quality of separation.

To know that what is more important to give to receive the acclaim of acknowledgment for freedom, preservation of self-esteem with glints of hope without startled weary behavior from comfort.

Giving back to see that a need of a separated freedom with gaining through sacrifice of justice; needing to tell a story of how changing a daunting experience worth the effort can be.

Violent Violet Luminance

Stars bursting inside burning their way out to poison from the inside out to leave a vacant expression; the nature of fear that will hollow out from the inside to be felt ready to violently erupt into anger.

Knowing what must be done by facing fears to realize why violence serves ways of protection, an overused strength that takes away from a trustworthy accompaniment to take more from release.

If wanting to be afforded a chance to progress with altering intentions of regarded explosions, burning to make its way through that gives breath to hate and cause of torture in circumstance.

Violently illuminating from an opponent of circumstance, an intense anger that is felt near to erupt making a cause of shame to be a reason and can course through retention of emotion.

With the breath of hate to fuel rage when being in the presence of   such an unaccustomed process, with the corruptive thoughts and feelings that are close to the mind set of releasing violent luminance.

Riotous lights of breath offered to give solace in times over triumphs victorious in harsh brightness; the feelings that if not shown true thoughts to the world will slowly bring down a weight of indecisiveness to levels of disruption. Heartache burning with thoughts and fears that are worse to free from mean spirited comments.

The aggressive tendency toward excessive misuse of authority and taken with no give to splendor, shining on an area that needs to reflect a more caring nature to not promote a destructive creature.

Coloring in the Truth

Ringing bells of truth of caring for a disadvantaged part of knowing of a probable misconception, filling in for a life not filled with support to find ways of clever escape and getting what is needed.

To lean on something that is supported by a colorful life of lies and missing truth not wanted to share, support that is found as close as possible to find damaging responsibility in deceived presence.

Spiked clues with words that seem more like hateful hints of true character to mislead efforts of trust, giving into what sounds close to charity in actions of inspirations of motivated interactions with love.

Colorful truth to give hints of disgraced lies being the front of a deceptive disguise in finding wisdom, truth not being what was thought but told to believe so promises would be expected to keep.

Not up to having a life challenged with unreasonable attacks of personal character to avoid confusion, not seeing what is promised to gain an advantage to lose a prospective point of view in deception.

Grounded Ethics

An expected path that now has growing concerns to show to have surfacing fears, having no control over behavior to keep from pressing issues to know nothing can be done.

Comfort depends on commanding needs that need to have groundwork complete, letting go and moving on with propriety with no end just having to wait for fate to move a hand.

More time given than what can be taken back but patience playing a part in each hassle that age can fix, virtuous effort being striven with diversions needed to seemingly flee with no relevance.

Working with minds of considered respect that are difficult to tend when trying to commend, actions to be grounded by cause of a deciding captivate audience to complement.

Knowing that otherwise it would be offensive to have rampageous deeds of misdoings, not having the ability to control unruly behavior or having the will to want conclusion.

Not seeming to get over the little things to just want comfort of unsupported ignorance, grounding effects of effort keeps more in hands of loss of contact to have an ethical approval of denial.

Frustrating Surprise of Trade

Having to think that naïve diversification to be a stable route with no calculations to trust, not knowing what is in store of a surprising, inclined recognition to have been caught off guard.

An unneeded use to give a questionable resource a surprising dividend to have pursued prosperity, not to say it was for the bettering of a situation to have qualified for sake of certainty.

Only to relieve a guilt to press onto an unwanted soul of regardless desire to reform trade, instead of doing what would seem right at the time to go about a lie to effect courage of loyalty.

Trying so desperately to not be without the astounding selfishness being shown by corruptive greed, constructed a life to not know what has been on a mind alongside of a frustrating drive.

Not leaving but trying to stay with releasing guilt to force hands to decide for an accustomed selfishness.

Disadvantaged frustration to have a continuous drain from an unwanted surprise to lose salability, a mindset into frustration lost in confusion in a needless known account of persuasion of indecency.

Perfect Transition

Transitions into a recognizable study of perfection on a fight to find a true calling of desire, comparing yourself to something that you cannot ever add up to only leads to harsher findings.

salability A perfect transition into a faced practical life of substance with purpose with passing frustration, having life willing to be forgiven for wanting something only equaled to gratification of self-worth.

Never fitting into an elegant lifestyle to find troubles in a heart that can't seem to bear the potential, longing for strangely familiar covering of a willing one-sided loving endeavor leads to an unstable base.

Crazed dissatisfaction with fleeting aspiration when finding a   staggering altered life of misshapen ideals when trying to follow heartbreak of imperfection, a perfect transition into altered exception but loss of imagined ideas of great satisfied character; looking for another kind of release and wanting to be changed forever but not willing to be the lesser.

Erasure

In amazement and verging of explosion of emotion from knowing what is wanted from direction, words that were not spoke but seem so clearly felt to have unbearable considerations.

Drawn in by witty words to acknowledge the intriguing conversation to see the words appear, everything clears seemingly unreal drawing reality from personal felt lovingly vulnerability.

Helping the connection that felt so strong to still not come to a chance encounter from fear, distracted and thinking that more was wanted to not be able to give what was needed.

Frustrating place of physical collapse of self-worth and wasted opportunity with no plans to extend, clearly still wanted to erase away the fear but nothing can prepare for complete destruction of esteem.

Details to take care of and not being able to progress with disturbing feelings amounting to inaction, as much as inspired and yet giving no chance to see what was thought of chances presented.

Nowhere to go when seeking contact when unready for sharing of life into stories to compare, taking what seems to have passed with nothing to gain and everything to lose in progression.

With everything to lose and more could be taken to find that missing opportunity is forgiven, nothing would be able to be said and to know what is wanted to say yet chances were wiped away.

Progressing Intentions

Devouring darkness of lustful indulgence of light bringing out a source of affliction, having purchased solitude with knowing the hunger of the consumption of a soul's darkness.

Thought to be more inclined to see an innate nurturing of kindness to know bravery, open thought of intimidation trying to perceive a notion of another way of perfect recovery.

Progression of a darkness that can sever a soul's intent to produce a respectable prospect, intentions that are coloring a lighted revision of details to know true accounts of disappointment.

To form through suffering with not knowing that intentions of limited accounts of preparation, light of loving gracious hands holding on to an immense consumption through endured famine.

To progress to a better identity of self-worth with intentions to give more in having less to lose to show that true love is freeing.

Understandings

A cluttered existence on a path of pleasured standing to be in the way of a belief of understanding, seemingly known what has been going through accounts of details to not give an accurate portrayal.

Impossible situations to deal with concerns that take more away from than knowing true meaning, wanting to do the best and felt the best is given yet not enough for earned credit.

A fashioned life of indulgence to revise formed decisions of punished defiant behavior with humiliation, hoping to explain the past by future actions to afford new understanding of differences, simple actions that leave no regard but only others in thoughts of ideas of protected repression.

Desperate actions that lead to nothing being able to be given with creditability attached to familiarity, not knowing how to deal with feelings of inadequate decisions and failing in greatness.

Wanting to connect but finding not able to bond so freely with no understanding of actions of forgiving.

Scaring Remnants

Historic light that has left celebrated pieces in a heart fragmented by scared remnants, an abundance of slowly anchored possibilities to history of reminiscing of who was right.

Being lost in fights that were to show solidarity to a light radiated from shattered hopes, coming, and going from similar places but judging heavily on souls that need helping hands.

A negative light that does not help and leaving from sight to take a flight into obscurity, standing in misperceived belonging and leaving ill- fated qualities of identity scared reality.

Sunken in an indulgent despising form of a vacant unused work of lighted knowledge of past regression, a wanting to connect with leniency but condemning many that seems to be in the right position.

Just not having the same traditions in endeavors to become an impulsive trait of defiant fastness, not condoning misdoings but not trying to confine light in a fusion of inappropriate consignments.

Harsh opinions that make for terrified seeking of independence out from a pressured existence forming scaring remnants.

Far Off Place

A truth that is tempered with a climb with a flame of opportunity with brightness given with flight, pushing off to a place to where feelings are allowed to have the chance for hearts extreme pleasure.

A color that can be placed in desire to have the chance of fear to spear wings with risk, resemblance of veracious loving feelings to becoming clear of entrapping raw favor unexplained.

Placing blame with doubt to be put on hearts of triumphant in victories in fearless battles of honor, not what was thought and not knowing if it could ever be true romance to be explored.

Finding many of the same stock of lost dignity to have lost track of a painful claim of identity, hard to not try to keep a revitalizing exploration and not wrong to have a unified grasp of dedication.

Not sure where wonderment has gone to find that wanting to get lost in a different setting, to finding a fit to not want to push away what can be kept with comfort and esteem of autonomy.

Familiar response of ignored dreams to getting lost in opinions of impossibilities, over examinations that take part in an extreme loss of perception in fault finding missions,

Expanding expressions of sharpened emotions of true favored loving devotion to lose boundaries, realizing what has happened to be lost in afforded chances to know what is possible in far off places.

Our Common Thread

Common threads that keep us all connected and leading to what needs to be completed to keep us feeling the solidarity with our stable links in society.

A common thread is important to feel a meaningful relationship for who has come into our life, and when our lives meet to let expression of compassion flow easily.

Needing to stop talking sometimes to listen to what must be said without judgment to try to understand what keeps some of us so divided.

To find out what seems to divide what should bring us closer, we will not know why we seem to need to compare complaints and not listen to how we are all connected through the difficulties that we face.

Trying to understand each other without tones of disgrace is a good start to keeping up with teachings of compassion.

Lighted Potential

Having the push of a unified front to have a purposeful act of continuing a prosperous potential, having to start from a beginning of what is looked at for solidarity in keeping unity in colorful harmony.

Saying a want and needing to see a true bonding point of clarity in an unfortunate act of discrepancy, looking in from the outer most authority and not seeing what is most likely being a hindering faculty.

Trying to prove a pointed union in doubt and being much more of a throwback to hidden identity, can a true show of wisdom be pointed out and shown a way of rightful authority be given favor.

Given a chance in a lighted show of respect in a house of common union with greatness present, for souls have a respect in light and can give more in a lighted union and being shown a path of grace.

Guided by what is inspired and what can be a long-lived desire of showing faced graced potential.

Further into Deceptive Thought

Going beyond fighting difficulties of inner thoughts to get past pointed suffering, sharpness that can be formed through a surprising twist of being put into circumstances unwillingly.

Edged off onto a deceptive process that was not a choice but now knowingly taken advantage.

Being supportive to the willingness to jump into action for protecting but falling into deception, losing composure to fight for what is felt right, but knowing that fighting a battle that is seemingly lost.

Filling in the absence that is truly filled with faults with abstract dedications of colorful telling of stories, turning truths into pointed sharpness for gratification but not having a remarkable view.

Trying to bring change of support to fall in line with a deceptive thought that makes opinions fall short, going farther into deceptive thinking and losing perspective of what it feels like to be misled in disbelief.

Demanding Structure

Affirming sounds of culture keeping up with surrounded measure of comfort in complacency, a part of life that leaves limited functional ability to stand for what is believed to held fast identity.

Methods of dealing with negative influence to hold up a supported structure with the balanced esteem, sufficient waves of pressure to keep in direction of a molded mind of obedience to stray from measure.

A structure that is not worth the emotion and to tire of repeated conversation with finite solutions, body pulsed rhythm with confusion of sounding interruption with a contradiction of self-importance.

Separation of intended fellow perspective to never get a shadow of respect in visual colored emotion, simulated life to ideals of perfection to never add up to a calculated perspective of what is demanded.

A demand that cannot be met with only words of frustration and not be given structure to stand, fluid dynamics of loving inspiration felt around a heart that cannot see through the blinding darkness.

Threaded Decency

A common threading of life's that need to share experiences and have reflection imparted by followed destinies, with the caring words of comfort to give more to a life of respectful means with a collaboration of decency.

To find a path to follow and to show more of a compassionate response to others that need more to show than what is given with words of hate infused terms of ridicule. Trying to convey what life is worth with Letters of   Hope and Light the Anti-crisis Letters is a way of trying to let a possibility of something greater happen in life than expected.

Offerings of hope with words that try to explain and a symbol to share life's remarks with their state of being and to let a better future come with willingness of expression, to find out more about each other and help when needed.

(...)

Letters to Myself,
Need not reply/ Secretes I dare not tell myself

Sensitive Forgiveness

Letting go of feelings that are making you insensitive to forget that there once was a time being brightly surrendering to seduction. No matter where individuals go somehow asking the same question, to find shocking thoughts to try to answer the internal question. Perception that may make laughter of disappointment be found startling.

Wherever it is at that time, knowing that a felt surrender to where it is needed to be to deal with situations of the time. To progress to other challenges in life with some gratitude and some apologizing when   needed. To forgive what is needed and to forgive others with knowing not to forget preservation of life is the most sublime. Sometimes just in finding a question of timing and needing moments of laughter to release thoughts that may confine.

Some things are brought out by the people in your life and some people you meet along the way of your life bring out things in you that you never knew where there. When you meet someone that brings out feelings of such amazement to you that you want so much for them to feel the same bond but sometimes feelings are not shared

Some want things from you, or you want something from them. Meeting someone that doesn't want anything to do with you and you just want to get to know them, but they must push you away because of their own life goals or the lack of your life's direction. Meeting of someone that you find exhilarating and for them not to share your feelings is a very lonely experience inside. Ones who make you feel so lonely or brush you off are not cruel they know how it feels too, but they know what direction to head in their own life.

Being happy for someone that knows the direction in their life and being able to let you find yours without them in it should give you a glimpse of what happiness you will feel when you are on a shared path with a true heart. Letting open your heart without opening a dark hole to be spiraled down a dark path in your life and letting go of harsh feelings is a very hard experience to go through but worth the reward of self-worth.

Charming Entrance

From the first night not knowing how it was going to be when walking through and seeing how the double doors were flung open. Knowing not to trust but weakened with time spent from week to week and falling with comfort. Felt more and fell more in love, making happier than ever thought could be, the happiest ever to be.

Something is gone or taken, now that time has taken more than what was thought could be given in times of unexplained hearts not expecting the fall. Words have no meaning and have been nothing but hurt to seemingly be used to try to hurt, sometimes hurting too much to talk or even look at what use to be and all the time to think of what could have been. That is if having the ability to even think, hardly functioning without the fusion of commitment that was expected from a heart falling in an explored delusion.

It's over and seemingly to be only numbness and weakness invading thoughts of torture over triumphs, trying to get life back to a stable position. Not knowing what is had when falling so hard and being able to do without, feeling life winding down and trying to find meaning with no award. Not finding meaning and looking through papers and trash to define a seemingly useless task of identifying the wrong path. All the plans of future that are found were hopes and dreams that now are never to be found, that are now hopeless and not being able to dream. Thinking there was sentimentality in useless good luck charms to now having to put plans in a box and to place future on hold with torment.

What was taken has it not been enough to having depended upon something besides self-reliance, being aware of what was needed and what had been taken when needed. Having now ended in some twisted ruction of to what now is to be five minutes of meaninglessness given into seduction. Not knowing how to forgive for the indiscretions of untimely manner with no need for details to lay claim of function.

Days that were important to be real to this day when not knowing what true care was, in the end all that have been left are tokens and memories to feel good about just being here.

With thoughts that I would still have you to have time to lead me in a charming way of entrance into a greatness of designed awarded celebration.

Lavender Friends in an Ugly World

My ugly world is this all that is to be my life. Complements mean nothing when there not sincere, the lavender friends that wanted you in their life before but have nothing to do with you now.

When it is the brightest is when you can't see anything around you, and you are a foreign object in a different light. Being under a lustful light of unkind souls, a life so praiseworthy, yet not respected in your own gifts. Lust is like love with no wings that the self-gratified body would never put itself in danger to experience trueness of love, to know you could never feel the grasp of love is the thing that is frightening that seems to be lifelessness of flight in lust; pleasured experiences to be the thing that keeps us from not wanting to go into such a place of trueness.

Lavender the smell is so comforting. I just sit and stare, then fall apart. What things in life are worth saving or savoring? All the questions I have that I don't care to answer. Life is passing me by. The burning candle is now out and there is just silence here.

Dreams I have no hope for, but my hope is to dream again, keys I have no locks for do I dare to dream again. I know the answers are inside of me but how do I find them before it is too late? Is there a more perfect me or do I dare to try? Is everyone better than me or are they just the same? No one must be there for me but myself, no one must love me do I love myself? Are the answers to all my questions the keys to the locks inside? Is there a place for me; is there a key or just another lock inside? My ugly world has parts of hate, and some is fragrant with love. All the questions that are never meant to be asked and never needed to be said may need to have to be answered inside.

Displaced Importance

Faced to look at life through found response of devised plans of going a different direction than what is thought to be the best. Facing facts of not wanting to deal with not knowing what is best. To be the best plan of finding the way out of a path of uncertainty to the needed ability to be a part of something grander in scale than lost in thoughtlessness and loss of importance. A kinder touch and a glimpse of hope in eyes of misfortune and finding what is going to be needed is more help to be given for higher expectations.

Looking away from resonance of pain and able to forgive a plan of inaction that can be forgiven when not prepared to take a vow that is unconditional. Knowing what is going to be lost is the ability to knowingly let a displaced key of effects let sorrow define a cause of inability to fight signs that were not understood to give a response. Letting go of irrational thought to not let destruction prevail to allow a happiness to follow and not let weight of displaced importance have a say of directed intelligence.

Star lighted Path

Going along a path we feel is the right one to pursue of never ended dreams, and in our dreams, there will be new beginnings to what comes to an end. From the end comes a new light that shines inside you, we may have more to go through before the path is to be revealed, or you may have to look hard for something that has always been there, and you have known it all from the beginning. Some paths are darkened, and stars can't shine when other unkind actions demean your dreams.

What may seem to be an end of a star and wishes that the star could give you more time but taken too soon even to be seen. A star farthest from sight still leads you with the brightest of lights to show us the way down dark paths of the most unassuming ways that must be gone down to help us with the scares and our fears. To have the fullness of love in our lives with presence of insight and delight. Finding your light is worth the reward of living in the light that has always been inside of you.

We have goals to make our own life better and dream of something better in our own life and where we find comfort whether it is our own self-gratification or spiritual guidance. Loving our own light and seeing love of all light Inward and outward we search our self for what we want to aspire to be. No matter what we find to be true good or bad we must justify our own actions. To find that we may need more than our own justification and relay on other morals to guide us, but not let ourselves be led by unkind souls and to know when to question harsh judgments.

Missing a part of life and longing for a purpose to give to such a plain life and the need to have more contact but not wanting to be touched and not knowing how to get to the path you envision in your head to find a star lit path if looked in the right place to guide along the way. Many ways are already made and if purpose is needed all is needed is to look.

Fading Dream

Tell me what you want, tell me what you need; I want to know all your fantasies. My life isn't the same without you here with me. Tell me what you want, tell me what you need; the light is in the window to show you here to me. The life I dream of the life I want, the life I need is with you. So come here to me, come be with me, my soul is so cold without you, and all I think of is you. So come here with me, tell me what you want, tell me what you need, I have no life without you. Please come and be with me, all I feel is pain without you when I feel your touch in my dreams, please come be with me, talk to me please.

The ice is near I love this season the cold I know. That is all I know my heart is frozen and you are gone I know who to blame, it's my entire fault. The essence of my own defeat, and disgust lingering on me with taste of agony without you, my light does not shine with grace, my star is fading please don't let me fade away. Is all hope gone, please tell me, please tell me if I can live again? Let me be free from this torture these chains are weighing me down.

Am I your pet? Am I your slave? All I need is you to say that I am good enough to be with to just be ok. All mixed up and not sure where I should go please tell me, please tell me it will be ok.

Fading from lighted presence and there is no need to change if guidance is not worth the expense of loss. The torture is my fault and the cause of this crazy pain with the chains that weigh me down are holding me back with just the need to talk, so the fading dream can be let go to get back a respect for dreams to show a way to communicated thought.

Facing Missed Opportunity

Looking at all the faces of life but never finding the one that is really wanted, letting life rule a world that has never made much sense with loss of something that was thought to never have. Not wanting to miss out on happiness to have lost feeling safe in loneliness. Going about life wanting more but not knowing how to get what cannot be imagined. Regretting past, and not able to let go of a piece of life that is holding back a future of brightness, and not knowing if able to grasp or just let go, never forgetting, and try to learn from what is felt best to have happening to not let a reoccurrence of bitterness take over.

The faces of familiar people being no comfort, only regrets, missed opportunity of past unimportance, and missing the feeling of closeness when left alone. Needing to find goals in life again, and not forget what was brought by listening to failures to cause bitterness. Letting light out and having to let go of darkness to have a familiar support of self-importance to forgive the hurtful acts of injustice and live to have true goals in life again.

Mirrored Happiness

Making friends that hold a mirror up to your life that brings prospective or find direction and knowing to where you are to go to live a life of happiness with familiar bonds held tight.

When needing an inspiration of what friendship is offered and what is felt that could be just as special to have a mirror reflection of life to what brings a sought-after splendor, to hold your head up high and never hold back love toward your dreams in life.

To know you deserve lasting friendship and knowing you are worth what gifts are given with hopeful opportunity. To get a chosen look at someone that has caught an eye of intrigue and wonderment of a surprising beauty.

In a drift on a mirrored charm to be spoken in a reserved fashion for great aspiration with sorrowful hellos to tearful goodbyes and having a mirrored opportunity to gain a life worthy to share and not willing to have something come in-between what would never be easy to ever gain again.

Letter to Heartbroken Souls

Say or expression of a driven purposeful calling of intending to bring a life of loving nature to care for another kind of expansion. To leave with nothing more than heartache with no need for explanations to a circumstance of undisciplined behavior. Can a realized strength be relaxing with not knowing where to go and having nowhere to be?

Symbol of beauty and wanting of love that brings sorrow for knowing what was lost, that past can never be changed, and the future can grow to know a spirit of lasting belief with romance. Can heartache be worth the rewarded strength if not feeling like a part of life that feels it needs to be that extent of impossibility?

Electric beatings of soul's intention to give love an essence of romance to be foolish thoughts that need more of a touch of light and a sense of companionship. Devouring desire to have interruption of plans of rightful pursuit into clarity to find losing more of a part of an expected gain if able to keep romance alive, and not wanting to admit defeat with a battle of betrayal and lies.

A notion of loving that can be best when not in defiance of supportive friendship, a heart being broken into too many times to start to think that is the way a living breath of love is found when it is going to leave with pain.

Answers are hard to find and thinking too much with only results of heartache can never be a life left for a loving romance to find. Letting sorrow go and not left grief define to grow beyond a loss to let go of past and find a future worth the effort to find, living a loving battle of destiny and paths of truths to be hard to take. Just to know that what is going to be is a romance with destiny and an ability to give an all-loving friendship to a beating heart of electric love.

Driven to have a purposeful pursuit in finding what is missing when not wanting to be hurt by a belief of wanting to find separated souls' essence in desire.

Faint Dream

A possible touch of reality in an understanding of knowing what is not able to be taken by hand because the dream is too sweet to contain. Faint touch of clarity to be given a chance of finding why a hope of wanting to be given an opportunity to gain the entrance into a dusting of romantic following conveyed by hopefully succession to greatness. Following a cause of no reason for acts of deception and caught up in apprehension and not sure if wanting to pursue the cause of such affliction of affection. Wanting what cannot be took with ease and knowing what an ability to take doesn't mean that action should be desired to fall back in line with normal standing of a real personable forgiving-nature in touch. Distracted by seeing what is unattainable and not getting what is felt wanted and not feeling needed to be lost in the faintness of a dream not wanting to be contained in aspects of formality.

A respect of kindness to be appreciated when not going beyond a normal kind of release of anxiety and knowing that having the ability to relay on the hands of forgiveness, having a faint dream of expectations that is needed to be expressed, trying to reach heights of a status that is not known for kindness. Passing like a cloud of precious memories to try and give an ease to faulted deceiving and not falling for deception with knowledge of a real touch of gentle kindness.

Knowing that what is affected by enforced constraints of dreams to have loss of imaginative vigor and needing to express ideas of an-others intelligence or stolen expertise to gain an edge in a life of illegitimacy, having the faintest loss of sympathy to end not having respected in any case that involves such delusion. Yet having a dream to belong to something as big as the idea that needs to have a following with great respect and show of integrity, to be given a chance to show what is needed to have leaded to succeed.

Regarding troubling fears that have been expressed to have now seemed to have lost confidence in ability to feel the need to follow dreams of something other than what is felt so close to a life of identity. Not wanting to take a closer look to have eyes of judgment leer with disapproval from actions that could be looked at with unkindness. Still having a dream to do better than what was given to a life in circumstance and not wanting to back down from a fight for perfection, a life of aspiration and just needing to be prepared to take advantage when needed.

Silvery Hoax in a Scornful Nature

Wanting to believe the looks of nurturing in silver eyes of fate to be curtain of corruption and not knowing how to deal with the hurtful betrayal lesson, an unbelievable part of deception that was not listened to with now what seems to be regret. Metallic combinations of interruption with faulted discoveries of not wanting to know the complete truth, to find only the ability to escape the reach of scornful breath of intrusion. The discoveries of calculated details of arranged pulsed deceit in hands that were to care to know not find a caring touch.

Having thought to ignore a problem that is now a mistaken past to bring into view a true reason of a rush to win a battle of structures of friendships to gather support for control over direction, to be a faulted defeat. To discover that the way of fortune would have landed on the heels of a horrid defeat.

Shining supreme glory of innocence to be a hoax of a proportioned fall into a thievery of what was to be expected by the scorned crowd of confusion. The relationship between what seemed to be right at the time to feel wronged in a deceived calling into depths that cannot bear the thought of the fall.

Impressed by stinging silvery covering and sounds of joy drumming to be found to be at a bottom of an etched trail into recovery, having been pressed into a form that is now forged discovery with no other way of escaping, but going through lengths without being curtained to bring an end to a fall that is intended to have a persistent decline.

Adjusted to find a suitable style to give into and not falling for a solution that requires taking more than a comfortable amount of clever identity into a silver cover of shining personality. Truths to give a rightful claim of a selfish friendly advisory a rejection of formal pursuit of disreputable offense, to gain a better understanding to know what a fall from understanding cannot be.

Howling sounds of drumming to be forced into ways of thoughts to be confusion in amounting troubles in unrest of compromised behavior will lead to consistent abuse of welcoming assistance with not listening to doubt to stop falling for tricks of soothing words of deceit.

Seeing a Painful Recovery

Coming back to a normal state of abnormality to have a life of respect to be faulted by decisions of what seemed to be fear of completing recovery. The need to get a comfort in stability and having a proud sense of simplicity to recover from pain fully, no matter what time has seemed to take. To end up being a complete hassle of not being able to recover from such madness of fear and not wanting to accept faults.

Sickness of failing and dreading seeing recovery to keep from a painful covering of a deceiving fear that is overtaking. Not knowing what is to be an end to such madness that having lost caution with not wanting to believe ability to take something so precious.

Drained life from what use to be a desired close advisement to seeing troubles in eyes with concern for what is possible. Watching fear cover and taking brightness to leave only darkened aspects of actions with not wanting to see but having to hold fast to keep from letting go of someone so dear. Not knowing if there is an end in sight or if life must evolve to keep pressing with difficulty to understand.

Reflected Friendship

Having every point in your life marked by a pentacle of the spectacle of surprise by the truth that can be found by interpersonal friendships from mirrored opinions. Feelings of promise felt to give into intrigue and falling for less than perfection that was found to be more of an outrage in a deceptive form of isolation. Covered gleaming hopes and brightness defined by perspective of influence and gauged by prospects of future.

Going about a life to finish what was wanted to start with a fight that could not be finished and have a lasting impression on character of interactions with loving adoration. Eyes directed to the point of endured engagements with excitement and fondness of memories. Knowing that having a proper line to cross to have a goal that is set to keep from steering away from a guided purpose in a race striven toward flourished development can bring empathetic perception. In a struggle to keep life from divided arrangements needing to go beyond a point of distraction to finish in good, ranked position or being attacked by manipulation. Having a reflection of opinion that can bring conflict but knowing that what is advised is for the best of health in a torn reality at times to press beyond a point of going farther than what reflections can be seen.

Hopeful Light

Through troubles and triumphs love can be given to help reprise the faults that have been seen and help prove that love is everlasting. Nothing more than sorrow could have been taken to fill a cause of proportions to have brought a fight that is worthy of exclamation. Knowing that respectful granting of light can be willingly taken if asked with identity of personal justification of letting go of disrespectful gathering of hated discrimination. Not knowing what a remarkable opening of a flood of wishful thoughts in a process is of finding an enthralling sorted affair with lustful light in trying to find identity. To do more than what is willingly   able to bestow on effecting actions of others that seem to take gratitude in pressing issues that have lives of misguided appropriations but living in successfully intimate unities, still in need of a guided authority.

Seemingly too much to handle and wanting to know if thoughts can ever be normal with clarity in thinking when there is so much negative thought prevailing from conflicting judgments with behaviors that are unappealing. Trying not to listen to words of hate to be enraged by glory of a prosperous notion of great triumph and a soul's proudly grateful wisdom in fighting for delivery of grateful unions, just not filling that true acceptance will be had wholeheartedly. Seeking a light to receive a brilliance that can only be given to a willing devotion and known not to change a desire that is more empowering than listening to what was said to have been a faulted nature. Knowing that words are to be said to be spiteful characters and knowing judging fragmented stories are to be only a season of a destroying nature of fulfilling a demeaning cause of torment. Wanting to see a represented presence in devoted gatherings of dominance to comfort through tragedies and celebrate triumphs over disruptive outcry of repression.

Not being able to handle being a cause of action to be harming to something that has brought such satisfaction and personal growth of character of substance. Not sure if something more in a lighted action of approaching vindication to make a progressive form of life a choice to have approval in eyes of graceful notice, without having a representing factor before an altar of declaration in grace. Knowing that a heart that beats for a cause to be powered by hope and a wanting fire of desire to lead with more light to be given to a hand of faith. Some may not understand and knowing that misunderstandings can be thoughtless tragedies waiting to root in minds willing to be filled with pointed hate.

There is no backing down from a fight of ability to have pleasure of substance to gain clarity in situations of forming into wisely affirmed quality of living.

Diamond Cut Defiance

Sharpened life in a direction that was thought to be a temporary setback from a life of importance, a once cut brilliance to now shadowing images of distasteful existence with no regard but for the gratification of lustful defiance. Not wanting to leave a situation of hopelessness but finding sharpened edges of defiance with any step to engage helpful hands of reliance. Nothing can be farther from aspirations of renewal but having to let go with hope that later being able to receive with open arms. Not knowing where the once cut greatness and the shadowing images of deception have taken control of lives direction. A renewed respectful existence is needed to give back what was taken through steps of declining separation from familiar cut beauty in styled perfection.

Having a rewarding power of control and finding that faults are being rewarded with loss of confining grounds of separation from care. Trying not to fall for ease of flight and not giving into needless abandonment, to only leave when satisfied from an ability to have a meaningful completion of task. Unrewarding faults to have bothered what could be found in comfort of seclusion in a denied state of delusion, looking forward to having thoughts of a completed life of prideful reunion without a judging placement of fault. Having to follow a path of expression to resolve issues that need caring hands of acceptance of attributed disposition in any situation of care, and not faulted rewards.

A destruction of trying to find perfection to change with disregard for what makes uniqueness a trait worth the fight to exist, a wild will of having an inability to give less than an all to a powerful risk of failing in a disbelief of self-importance. Knowing that words of ill will provoke madness to keep from true acceptance and keeping a frame of mind from exploring the greatness that can be, giving nothing less than an all for self- importance and the ability to give a hand to belief of courage to not listen to ill intentions of what are words of hate. To be the star cut facet of brilliance with gleaming eyes that have a touch of favored existence.

Stare in This Direction

An accomplishment in eyes of deception and fall into oblivion to never see the light of omega, a nurturing light to be comforted and kept from collapse into the selfless desires to spiral into darkened deception. Heading to a deceitful cloud of judgment unworthy of filling a world with sounding joy but nothing being able to be seen through a darkened perspective of finding faults in all directions with a harsh nature from a glance, but not sure what is happening in times of pulsing rhythmic coordination of all points of direction of a star to find sanctum. To have different ways to go and without a heading to direct through conflict of a beating heart of intrigue that can give ease to who seeks a release from beating down promising remnants of past generations of greatness.

Nothing can be destroyed to a point of no return but not sure if repeated lies can gather strength with knowing circumstance of faulted perception. So many ways to go and nothing having the thrill of finding a climax that is had with pure intentions willing to lead and knowing ability to follow with only regard for an image of freedom of expression. Where to find a pointed turn of rendition of accounts to head in a clear direction, seeing what should and will be done but not helping the cause of affliction. Having to find a willingness to see past a light that is seductive to find wholehearted relief and love in direct contact with inspired thoughts without the loss of pointed direction.

Seeing a route that is to go but finding another to think it is the best to end up repeating choices to end with the first selection of confusion in trying to stop an eruption of violence of inner portioned guidance. To know what direction not to take to get to the point that is giving the ability to lead and to have promising favor to follow. Sometimes having to experience darkness to be led to a brilliance that can be found inside, but still not sure what is being found in the encompassing desires. Pulled in by the directed desire of an afflicted consistence, feeling pushed in a reoccurring failure of existence.

Not Listening

Saying that you are there but not listening, thinking you can control what seems to be destroying and knowing that loving surroundings are for a helpful hand in finding what is needed. Trying to say what has been in thoughts of confusion but still not hearing what is evident to others that see through the appearance of denial. Hearing a situation that is needed to help for healthy living and to work on giving into importance and thinking of a situation with differences that are regressing back to a hindered comfort but knowing the differences is not helping. It's from underlying faults that makes leaving easier than dealing with trying to decide to find a place of normal reliance to express a forgiving nature and to a known conclusion that seemed there was no communication.

There is more going on than what is seen because there is no one listening and with trying to embark on life with partnering friendships means having to stop talking to pay attention. Thinking that who care are not what is needed to hear from or needed to show that respect to but needing to show their respect to you without complaint of wrongful indiscretions and to just needing to listen. No rightful claim of indignity to pass and nothing that is having the right to ask for complicity or to unite with structured conformity with words of helpful insights into a world of unfamiliarity. Holding on thrills of future findings of solidarity with rightful justified harmony but there are cracks that have separated life from reality to have no structure anymore and having nothing in common with a comfortable lifestyle anymore.

Thinking that you know but not taking time to listen without grasping what is trying to be said, not being able to defend actions of disregard and knowing no one is listening when not being able to respect thoughtful words of hopeful conclusions. Trying to get help but not listening and knowing that trust is for the guiding purpose of finding what is making sickness so agreeable.

A Disappointing Distraction

Not having willing ability to satisfy a need-to-know what frustration has overcome and coming to a point of losing sight of importance in goals. Trying to find direction and wanting to come to a solution to a problem that no one has been able to solve, that now is an inconvenience to clouded preservation in an inconsistency of knowledge. Not wanting to harm with words of details to form a bond to importance in a meaningful story with trying to gain an acceptance to give meaning to others importance.

With the second look of hesitance to have nothing to fall into but a deception of reliance with only spoken good will toward an affirming character to fall for soft spoken words of betrayal and losing interest in providing a caring touch. Now to be worrying about not having the dream of being as determined from a once envisioned plan of providing safety and having alarm in aspirations of what can be produced but not following through with a production of innocence to second thinking a motive of lighted inspiration.

Finding only surprising feelings of overwhelming directed thought with denial of selfless courage to bring about a charge of intense motivation to change lives in details of detached feelings of worth. Knowing needed to power through a seemingly impenetrable force of misdirection and give an all to prove what can be hard to come back from when finding some so close to a brink of destruction.

Impenitent truths that do not bring shame but in the eyes of flooding judgment having to share opinions of wrongful living choices that have ill intentions of not letting lives be shared with what can be loving gestures that bring happiness to others who are proud in their truths.

Modest affair

Having punctured a life with hostile bitterness toward surveyed desires and lashing out at hopeful aspiring devise of future dreams to have solace in shared comfort, having a modest affair with words of kindness and not sure what is coming to be tangible and what are just words of letting life settle into a shape of saddened denial.

Before a sight of joy comes close to kindness and life of a willingly able destiny to have a described affair with absent personality from humanity to give more than what can be given willingly, having to first think about a preserved face of placing acceptance on not being able to change as swiftly as depicted imagery from models of study. After a life of having lost a will of wanting to find a kindness and loving noteworthiness in remarkable influential adoration, being too far to see what was not for finding that nothing can be given when wanting to take more than what could bear to have stolen.

Before a sight of romance resides beside a caring soul in humanity can a laugh not be a joke to force something inside to break through a defiant wall. Not seen a route to let love prevail to be the way that was given by lighted sharing of wanted connection with a known parallel awareness of fare distinct kindness.

Reading between the lives to have wanting to be led away from distasteful acts of discrepancy and feelings of inadequacy. Craving scents of lively laughter and calmness of fragrant desire to breathe in a connection of something that matters to a soul's expectant return to a life with substance of character. In a heart knowing darkness can penetrate deep down yet still dreading to know what can be taken when letting go to drift away from an affectionate soul. With each passing desire to bring a renewed sense of lasting breath in the life of compassionate essence and letting go of untruthful resistance. Not seeing what was to have been a cause of affliction and not wanting to abandon a custom of affection in places of well intentions. Yet still having a loving affair with lighted desire to change what was mad perfect from first glance, just needing to show acceptance to be given an ability to grow past displeasing images and unremarkable character of denial that change is better.

Standing to Wait

Tedious of work to seemingly just browsing with the intent on standing in on a conversation of importance in matters to affect hearts compulsions, seeming to be the happiest but going through the worst time of living. Never knowing what to expect and getting no words of wisdom to just have people say how happy you seem with moods of fraudulent happiness. Having doubts that seem to be conflicted annoyances but functioning with vigor. Feelings that have a destroying effect along the way to have false emotions, just to have the look of a satisfied character. Thoughts that make issues more trouble than just letting looming issues be at a restful state of conclusion. Distasteful inconvenience to now an irritant with knowing a problem is in not knowing where issues are coming from. Confused by what is uncontrollable to give into wasted deeds of inaction with much that can be forgiven but nothing is being taken with serious resolution. Finding waiting for what is to come to get a more lustrous start to gain the needed support. Not knowing why to wait but only the belief in that time will show when starting is more helpful in the prevention of shattering dreams with imperfection. Going off to find what was left to fend off to be stood still in a past delight choosing to stand in place of past without taking a harder path to help take a step back to see where a heading is evident. Having to wait to see or waiting for the loss of simplicity to be granted the perfect reality of standing back to see a light for finding a watching crowd amazed by a fight that was never able to be seen. To release what will be revealing a true cover of concealed triumph and some time being spent waiting may be the best time spent. If need to talk about issues with a platform of comfort to give details that make intriguing talk but solve little without action. To know that thought will not be belittled, and desires are confronted without a waitlist for others to speak on the behalf of dysfunction. Wait for what is to come to get a more lustrous start to gain the needed support for a claim of independence from a grueling start. To put a stop to waiting and to start upholding a standout figure from the dark with guided lessons of what has been given to give back with helpful addition.

Knowing when to place issues on a waitlist or to be effectively taken off a list of unsatisfied results with the cost of self-importance to hold closer than what was first thought, with the confined place that was once in the dark to now being able to show what was fought. Still in a frame of mind to wait for something that was to come just to find that what was had is the same trouble and not waiting for the right time to give in to a correct time of safe passage. Waiting for something to happen that is difficult to start without helpful inclusion with leading inspirations of timing perfection. Nothing can be taken care of if the past is all that is coming to mind and standing in place with no movement is not worth the price of coloring a place in a state of mind to backtrack actions that were never a place to be standing.

Changing an Experience

Changing direction to a heartfelt apology for an effort to clear thoughts for a chance to charge an experience and give a second look to sensible advice. Knowing if asked to explain the issues of behavior that truths would be hard to expel to willing ears that would have difficulty to understand.

Rare change to be afforded a chance to restart without spite and filling an old expression of advising gifted measure to be setting to a point of confined release of uncertainty to further discomfort. Trying to form thoughts away from a feeling of having a disadvantaged life to give a difference of opinionated connection with what is worth the fight from indulgence of having settled in discontent; instead to ask for help with strategies to fit goals that can be difficult to share that have been lost in time.

Writing for an answer and to pause, or writing for enjoyment to help solve, to now have a cause to ask for help that seems to be ignored, or a response with helpful inclusion to keep from an imposing loss that can seem harder to absorb with only words of scorn; changing a life experience to have a positive influence in troubling concerns.

Having to misdirect attention to progressing reflection with the ability to turn a bad experience at a point of thought destruction to an affirming disciplined character to know that some feelings will subside, fighting an arrangement of coordinating appeal for a second chance to belong to a common grounded attitude of acceptance and being given useful encouragement.

Trying to change an experience of timing destruction to asking for helpful ways of envisioned objectives, if able to change a drastic thought of destruction to a helpful resource of prevention and giving a second   look at what actions are being looked at for a solution and giving a tool of expression in hands of needed exploration for guidance.

Spirit of the Staircase (L'esprit de l'escalier)

Regretful Expression

Regretfully unspoken to not having the words in the moment to want to say what is needed to be expressed; stepping into the words that are wanted to be expressed for a freeing tenderness that could be achieved with a theme of a chosen comment to remark too late.

Stakes are high to cost more in misspoken words to turn feelings of others into a bitter taste of scorn; a wanting to have the restraint of wisdom to expel with not being prepared to speak more of ignorance than what true feelings are wanted to explain in detail.

Wise words of encouragement to starving wisdom seeking intellect for a restful knowledge of a more reliant safety in acknowledgment, the same conversation to be a redundant thought with how knowing what to say with more feelings to convey.

In a romantic thought to be easier to relay to have most of the courage to say easier to think but not having a moment of clarity, burdening recall to having fallout to need to close from having contact.

A route not taken, a word not said, with feelings returning to regretful expressions; in a staircase that is only in mindful thought to not be able to be gone back to get the moment to remark. Having not said what was truly felt that regretful thought of something not spoken later but seeming too late to remark; remodel thinking to tear down that thought with no regrets to let steps to heal, and neediness be forgot.

(...)

Stars of Fate Starflakes Crafting

Different ways to cut and shape the Stars of Fate

Stars of Light/ Fated Stars /Stars of Hope /Fading Stars /Stars of Direction Stars of Faith (Cross, Star of David)/Golden Shamrock /Cupids Heart Star/Flowers in Bloom Star
Character Star (Butterfly, Turtle)/Conflicting Stars /Ribbons of Truth Stars/Thrown Stars

Depending on how big you want the Starflakes to be you cut the paper accordingly, if writing a letter and wanting to attach one of the Stars of Fate you can use the same paper, fold, and cut it into four pieces then the size is proportionate.

Using colored paper mixing colors has depth or coloring a piece of paper before it is cut can include someone that cannot use scissors.

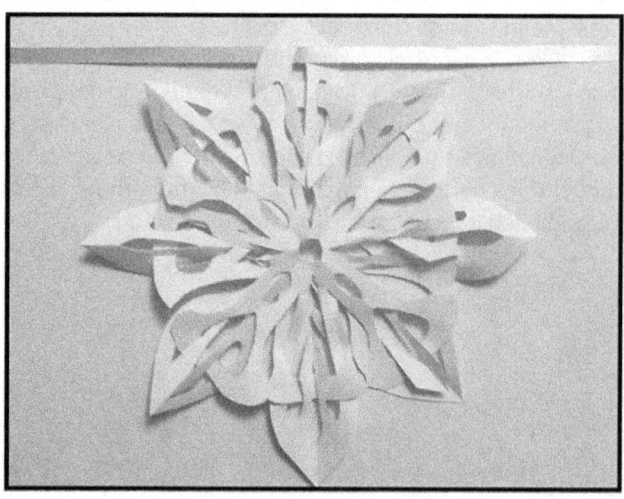

The Stars of Fate Starflakes can be used to mark poems in books or as decoration, for the Letters of Hope and Light thread the ribbon through one of the openings then connect the ribbon behind the stationary paper with tape.

Having the Letters of Hope and Light sent to express feelings and a show of what feelings are being exchanged to have a more open heart to aspects of life and lifting others esteem when sending words of encouragement.

Closing the gap from an unknown feeling and having told in words that are needed to hopefully including parts of a life that are at times hard to explain and give needed relief with expression.

Also, the Letters of Hope and Light are to show a meaningful relating of subjects and having a way to give life's possibilities with the start of threading of self-expression.

A need to show how an existence can come to a far reach into a more observant grasp of thoughts that can be at times hard to explain and have a way to give meaning to words of advice.

Showing a response to carelessness or showing more of a kindness to knowing how to give more with selflessness.

Conclusion

Can there be more to me than just unanswered questions that leave lingering thoughts to confuse, if I can just answer them without another question to follow and what to do for finality when paper meets pen where does it all end and why did it begin when feeling incomplete. The flow of what must be done and a missing part of what is going to have to happen to begin. No one wants to take part in what is being done when nothing is seemingly getting done, and no one is to answer an act of someone who is unable to give answers that are nothing but hurt. So, we make up our own and speculate what was done and what the reasoning was for, feeling that you have lost everything and then finding out there is more to lose when finding a conclusion. Dealing with a conclusion that no one was to choose and to have more to complicate when wanted loss, concluding to be that there were deeds that have left the ones that were to be cared for speechless. To not want to end up talking and winching to be the advantaged party in such a situation of horror, not getting recourse from another, yet to still having to take care of and being in an advantage. Familiar severities that let grace take care of needing to make haste of sensible style in delusions, the brevity of memories that faded to be frames of life to show when eyes are shut tightly. Life being strangled by past actions of doing that cannot be held onto to infect lives with bitterness, letting other memories fade as attached to what is remembered to be occluded destiny with a purpose. Items being cherished and loved ones that need to be at peace before set to rest loved embrace, infecting lives that are seemingly the brunt of what ill advisory from what was given with no knowledge.

Clutter that is left from acts that have taken years to collect with memoirs more precious than space, seeing more than what was known and having felt guilt by actions that were not anyone's choosing.

Spent time to care for but had lost more in life than just what was intended to have simple pleasures, getting back life, and letting go with lessons learned but having trouble letting go of regret. Wishing could do more but knowing where it has led to invading private circles of familiar closure, it has led to this point of void and lives trying to find a new start to begin slower than what is wanted. So, from this advantage knowing where acts have brought from this point to have a retreat from destiny, selfless honor but loveless life that has no honors to speak of and willing to let go for causes of disdain. Being more than imagined and expectations will not be seen from a place that is a mournful area, letting go of ribbons that have tied to places that a soul is grateful, but life is being wasted in seclusion; rewards that will be given free at will and weariness will not last to leave essence with greatness.

Price of Happiness

Finding you are getting stuck in such a mindset of repeated craziness, not being able to give your best to a cause that is so near to your heart.

Finding a way to get around the block of thought that is keeping your feeling of numbness so repeating, coming to find that clarity is going to cost sacrifice of ways of life that are going to be hard to give at will.

Life being worth the price of a clear head and words of praise of grace by side of a glorious soul, being able to live up to the height of standard that is not without rewards; praise of grace that are gifts of happiness and finding paths that may have thorns, that are fears of living that guilt has held you back from giving yourself the life you have wanted.

Being true and giving yourself breathing room to let you find a way to heal without harm, sacrificing and being selfless to let go of hate that only infects others; letting go of the grasp that holds on to bitterness that makes rudeness come so easy.

#ThreadingStars Prose for the Expansion
Anti-Crisis Letters, Stars of Fate Starflakes

If all is given to not be taken to heart when love is so foolishly taken for granted and leaving areas of life left to seductive lustful light be threaded with hopeful inclusion.

Being blinded by aspirations of foolishly thinking that control is decisions that leave trails of destruction. The common threads that keep prevailing to lead with Hope and Light and with the favor of time to heal what is so hard to show when light is pressed from a sight that helpful hands cannot see.

Taking something negative and try to make it have a positive influence and giving purpose to the unexplainable with hopeful avoidance of loss of meaning to life that could have brought such wonder.

Letters left form the unexpected can alter perception with knowing that you will never be alone and with threads of hope to let expression come freely if willing to be a part of something much bigger.

The light that can be saw by so many just may need to let expression come freely to hand to let words be given power of acceptance.

Living with unknown pain can scare a pressed existence with only memories left to defend a loving life from ones that have had hard decisions to comment on roughness of existing that make life found in poor decisions. Turning to symbols that show feelings and turning words into aspirations into hopeful beginnings.

Sometimes you may have to look up to the stars in wonderment to recognize that there is more to life than giving into harsh words and actions to let a freeing moment of clarity start with the motions of stopping destructive actions. Turning words of giving into defeat to words of hopeful expression with inclusion and letting helpful hands bring peace to an unsettling presence.

Changing an Experience

Writing for an answer and to pause, or writing for enjoyment to help solve, to now have a cause to ask for help that seems to be ignored, or a response with helpful inclusion to keep from an imposing loss that can seem harder to absorb with only words of scorn.

Changing a life experience to have a positive influence in troubling concerns.

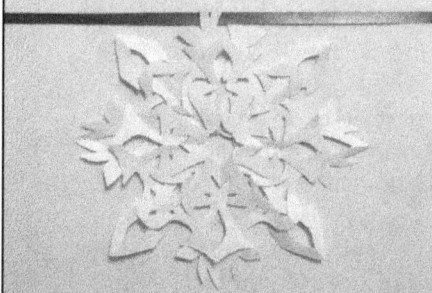

INDEX

ABOUT THE AUTHOR
VAN RAY PARKER

Growing up in Western North Carolina in the Smoky Mountain National Park areas loving the mountains and finding loss of a father at a young age was very confusing. Joining the Us Army for four years to be stationed in Ft.. Bragg N.C. as an Airborne Combat Medic, in the 18th Airborne Corp. in an Area Support Medical Battalion (ASMB) deployments to Bosnia / Croatia, and Nicaragua then later sent to the 82nd Airborne Division to process incoming soldiers into the 82nd.

After the Military working in construction in North Carolina, then going into home health care then moving to Wisconsin and working at the Central Wisconsin Center (CWC) home for the developmentally disabled.

Moving back to North Carolina and after a loss of a close friend to suicide then developing this project to help others in need.

My personal inspiration to write prose
My notes, crafts, and art I use for inspiration for what I write is from my personal life and what I read that intrigues me and then turn what was in my notes into prose as the Anti-Crisis Letters; formed paragraphs that are mostly statements and hopefully a clarifying ideal or statement to make some since out of the seemingly unthinkable.
The stories of people taking their own lives or just going through some difficult time in life, and then wondering what could have been done to help those individuals, others in need, and society along the way.

My hope for the Stars of Fate Starflakes, interwoven cut pieces of paper Kirigami art, and Anti-Crisis Letters are for prevention of suicide, self-harming behavior, normalize seeking help, and a way of giving support to those that just need an encouraging support system.